Praise for
JUST SAY YES: Create Your Dream Business and Live Your Dream Lifestyle

Jim Palmer has been a consistent positive force in my life: As a friend, a business coach, an author, and by demonstration of how he runs his business and lives his life. Jim's last book, *DECIDE* hit me like a ton of bricks. I was living in "Squishyville" and Jim's advice allowed me to "Just Say Yes!" – pulling me out from being stuck to feeling real freedom from my business again. Jim is a one-of-a-kind success coach you've just got to listen to.

~ Craig Valine
Marketing Performance Strategist/Coach
www.EMPResults.com

Life is short, so we need to be mindful of how we live it, without regret. *Just Say Yes* gives clarity to the point that you can live your best life... and you can do it NOW! I know the heart of Jim Palmer is to infuse life into you, so you too can live a life of your dreams! Are you ready to *Just Say YES*?

~ Michelle Prince
Best-Selling Author, Zig Ziglar Speaker &
Self-Publishing Expert
www.MichellePrince.com

Every entrepreneur and business owner can improve the power of their YES. Jim's insights, as always, deliver a real punch to those who may hold themselves back with head trash and fears. Inside *Just Say Yes*, Jim shares how to create a pivot in your results by developing the confidence and courage to pursue your biggest dreams.

~ Melanie Benson
Profit Amplifier for Thought Leaders,
Visionary Entrepreneurs, and Change Makers
www.MelanieBenson.com

Having read several of Jim's books, I was anxious to jump into his latest work *Just Say Yes*. Without opening the cover, I knew that I was in for a treat. This is a book full of life and business wisdom that you probably won't be able to put down – and you shouldn't! Start by buying it, then read it from cover to cover. The nuggets of *Just Say Yes* wisdom in every chapter are worth many multiples of the price paid for this book! I enjoyed every minute that I spent reading and learning from Jim's knowledge, and I am sure you will too!

~ Clinton Wasylishen
Quick Wins Business Coach
www.QuickWinsBusinessCoach.com

Want to make it **BIG** in your business and live your dream life? Then start here by reading *Just Say Yes!* with Jim Palmer. Anyone who wants to "go big" fast needs to get on the boat and read this book!

~ Marty McDonald
Author of *Great Beer is Not Enough*,
CEO of Bad Rhino
www.BadRhinoinc.com

After reading Jim's seventh book, it has occurred to me that the number seven is the number God uses as perfection in the Bible. This book is a perfect example of what all of us entrepreneurs go through. It's like a daily seven-step process, and he nailed it. A great read for anyone wondering what to do next and where to go with their business. Just keep going, don't give in, and don't give up!

~ Dr. Raynette C. Ilg N.D.
Olive Branch Wellness Center Inc.
www.olivebwc.com

When you *Just Say Yes*, magical things happen that seem almost accidental. This book shows you how to move past fear to forgiveness, and from stuck to success. Using the principles that Jim describes in his book, I've been able to be, do and have more of everything in life – clarity, connections, money, confidence, resilience, and accelerated growth. And it all started with a "yes."

~ Stephanie Frank
International Best Selling Author, *The "Accidental" Millionaire*
www.stephaniefrank.com

Jim and his words of wisdom just get better and better! This book is not only one of the most motivational books, it is filled with tons of Jim's personal stories and other stories of just saying yes, all the way to great success and a life full of adventure. Jim is so real and honest. You cannot read this book and not be inspired to join his following and *Just Say Yes!* His approach to *Just Say Yes* is how I got my first book written and how I tripled my rates in one year. I never would have done it without Jim's coaching approach outlined in this book to growing a successful business.

~ Natalia Volz
Coach, Author, Speaker
Founder, www.PassingThroughGrief.com

This is a biased review based on facts about Jim Palmer! Jim Palmer is the most candid, practical, and heart-warming coach I have worked with. He has years of experience in business and in coaching "special" entrepreneurs like me, helping everyone soar to new heights if we choose to *Just say Yes!* In this book, Jim shares his insights on how to deal with fear, how to get rid of limiting beliefs, and how to fast track to success. The book is full of stories, some very personal, designed to help you reflect, understand your mental blocks, and break through to your new business goals. I highly recommend this book and hope you reach out to work with Captain Jim Palmer, The Dream Business Coach.

~ Dr. Emily Letran, D.D.S.
Certified High Performance Coach
Exceptional Leverage Coaching
www.DrEmilyLetran.com

This book was "compelling, entertaining, practical, and inspirational." Another textbook that belongs on every entrepreneur's desktop. Practical lessons and tips to guide you to success in an easy-to-follow format. The unique thing about Jim is that he tells you like it is, and challenges you to step up and do something. Just do it : *DECIDE* and say "Yes"!

~ Dr. Tom Streko
www.DrStreko.com

Just Say Yes motivates entrepreneurs and small business owners to stop making excuses and achieve their dreams. I love this fantastic book.

~ One-Click Lindsey
Web Strategy Expert
www.TrafficAndLeads.com

Jim's done it yet again with his latest book *Just Say Yes!* Inspiring and motivating, helping you get ready to take action and of course *"Just Say Yes."* Jim shares his wisdom and experience in this book, so you can start to apply it to just about anything you find challenging in life.

~ Kate Bradbury
Administrative Consultant
Admin Icons, Inc

How many times have you thought... "Wouldn't it be amazing to do (fill in the blank)?" You really want to move forward but life happens, and seven years later, it's just one more regret on the list. You're trudging along getting by or even doing well, but there's that pit in your stomach of what could have been had you just went for it and said "Yes." Well, the great news, inside this book, you'll discover it's not too late. You'll also enjoy the stories that bring to life the key insights and principles to help you say "Yes" to the right things for you and your dreams. Soon, it will be others looking at your lifestyle and saying... "Wow, wouldn't it be amazing to do what they are doing?" If you have big dreams but haven't reached them all yet, this book is for you!

~ Matt Sellhorst
Creator of the SPLASH System™ for Boat Dealers
www.BoatDealerProfits.com

We all have that "YES" in us. Sometimes we just need someone to help us realize the potential of it. Jim's powerful stories and business lessons will get you to *YES* and beyond. I am a testament to his wisdom as my business grew more in the past year than the past 10 combined.

~ Stacey Riska – "Small Business Stacey"
The Small Biz Marketing Specialist
www.SmallBizMarketingSpecialist.com

This book hit the nail on the head, and the advice about fear and forgiveness really hit home. Removing fear from stopping you from new adventures (and opportunities for growth both personally and financially) and forgiving yourself for any bumps in the road is a huge hurdle to get over. If someone can even take a nugget of info from this book, like minimizing the head trash and "what if" game – it's worth the read. Saying *YES* to the book and business and life can truly bring your dream into fruition. I know, because I've done it! Thanks Jim.

~ Lyndsay Phillips
CEO & Founder of
Smooth Sailing Business Growth
www.smoothbusinessgrowth.com

Jim's latest book, *Just Say Yes*, is my personal favorite! He will inspire you to make the changes you've been craving, personally and professionally. Even if you're feeling fear or disappointment for past mistakes, he supports you through it. I said "Yes" to Jim's coaching and have been truly blessed!

~ Carmen Torres
CEO & Chief Specialist
www.MyHRSpecialist.com

One of my great blessings as an entrepreneur has been having Jim Palmer as my mentor and guide since 2009. One of my great joys has been observing Jim's own metamorphosis and journey, as I first got to know him during the "revenue free" year he talks about in *Just Say Yes!* His story will inspire, captivate, and motivate you to stop waiting for the time to be right to experience the business and life you know you deserve. Not only will you feel confident to

"just jump," but Jim will also show you HOW to grow wings, so you soar higher than, up until you, you believed possible.
Pick up Jim's book right now – it's a short, easy, engaging read – and feel inspired to *Just Say Yes!* to that thing you "shoulda" been doing all along. You'll thank yourself for doing so!

~ Adam Hommey
Founder, The Business Creators' Institute™
www.BusinessCreatorsInstitute.com

Just Say Yes is chock full of golden nuggets. Just saying yes has always been a part of who I am, mainly because I was afraid of missing out on the opportunities that might be missed. Many refuse to say yes because of fear, or the unknown, just saying yes, this is where your true rewards lie. Read this book!

~ Dave Negri
http://contractorssecretweapon.com

Jim's wife, Stephanie referred Jim to me for personal training services at my gym. Jim hired me to help build his strength and relieve back pain, so he can enjoy his adventure on their Floating Home. Little did I know this became a "who's helping whom" moment. Through casual conversation, he suggested I consider attending his Dream Business Academy to learn how to market my gym. Between the Academy (which was the best business investment I have ever made) and subsequently turning to Jim for business coaching, I have a new outlook on my business. Instead of guesswork, I have a clear objective to what will bring me more clients, retain my existing clients (the best part), and end the wasted (and expensive) effort of weak marketing. Here's my big takeaway: There are a lot of business coaches/experts/gurus out there all claiming to have the solution to becoming successful. However, few, if any, have the honesty, flexibility, and a truly genuine attitude to help you that Jim Palmer has. No matter what business or business idea you have, you are doing a disservice by not hiring this man as your business coach and mentor.

~ Andrew Clauser
Personal Trainer and Owner of
Fit This Way of Chester Springs, PA
www.fitthisway.com

Just Say Yes is brimming with toughness coated in love, just like the author. I like a book that gets straight to the point and Jim's point is this: You have a life to live (and a business to run) and you either just say yes to the opportunities that come your way or face regret later down the road. Being scared or feeling uncomfortable is not an excuse for not saying yes. Read this gem of a book and then *Just Say Yes* to whatever your heart tells you to do next.

~ Lin Eleoff
Gutsy Glorious Living
www.GutsyGloriousLiving.com
MyFreedomMastermind.com

When I **DECIDED** I wanted a Dream Business as part of my encore-career, I went looking for a trustworthy coach with superior marketing and branding know-how. Having attended the Dream Business Academy and having been coached by Jim, I can tell you he delivers on both – and that he is as authentic as he is inspiring. With *Just Say Yes*, Jim not only leaves his own success tracks you can begin to navigate today, he also hits on all the elements needed to create a life of greater impact and significance.

~ Peter Atherton
President and Founder of ActionsProve, LLC
www.actionsprove.com

The title of this book is the reason I am so quickly writing my own book. Being coached by Jim Palmer took me saying yes and applying his years of experience. *Just Say Yes* and see how your life can change.

~ Tracy Ricks
Owner - The Donut Shop
www.thedonutshoprincon.wixsite.com/smile

Jim has a way of bringing what you may think "complex" down to simple, understandable concepts. Jim has a passion to help those who really want to "create their own flight plan" and *Just Say Yes* shares those lessons on how to get clarity on your mission in a simple and coherent way!

~ Dave Sanderson
Dave Sanderson Speaks Enterprises
TedX Speaker,
Author of *Moments Matter*,
coach and former head of security
for Anthony Robbins

Do you know a friend, colleague, or perhaps a group
that would enjoy and benefit from the information and strategies in this
book?
If so, we're happy to extend the following volume discounts!

Just Say Yes:
Create Your Dream Business and Live Your Dream Lifestyle

$19.95 U.S.

Special Quantity Discounts
5-20 Books - $16.95
21-50 Books - $13.95
51-100 Books - $11.95
101-250 Books - $8.95
251-500 Books - $6.95

Call or e-mail today to order bulk quantities
610-458-2047
coach@getjimpalmer.com

JUST SAY YES:

Create Your Dream Business and Live Your Dream Lifestyle

By Jim Palmer
Your Dream Business Coach

With a Foreword by
Adam Urbanski
The Millionaire Marketing Mentor

Dream Business Academy
Dream Business Coaching & Mastermind

JUST SAY YES: Create Your Dream Business and Live Your Dream Lifestyle

Published by Success Advantage Publishing
64 East Uwchlan Ave.
P.O. Box 231
Exton, PA 19341

Printed in the United States of America

ISBN: 978-1546578864

Cover design by Jim Saurbaugh, JS Graphic Design

This book is dedicated to my family,
Stephanie, Nick, Steve, Jessica, and Amanda.

Table of Contents

Foreword

"What you can do, or dream you can, begin it; boldness
has genius, power, and magic in it."
~ Johann Wolfgang von Goethe

Dear Reader, (or potential reader, if you're still browsing):

After working with thousands of entrepreneurs, I
discovered there are three reasons why many fail to achieve their
dreams. The first is the "confidence gap." What stops most people
from building their Dream Business is not the "I can't," but the "I
won't." The former simply indicates a lack of initial resources or
skills, which – as you'll soon learn – can be easily overcome. The
latter is deadly. The "I won't until" is a result of self-imposed
limits and lack of courage to act now.

The second reason people fail is asking the wrong "HOW
DO I?" question. Too many budding and successful business
owners are stopped from reaching their full potential because they
ask "HOW DO I DO IT?" ("It" being whatever their big goal is at
the moment.) While it's a valid question, it's not nearly as
important as your answer to this one first: "HOW DO I NEED TO
THINK DIFFERENTLY?" And that is why you need to read this
book.

Truth be told, after my initial excitement about being asked
to write this foreword subsided, I had only one question on my
mind: "Why did I *Just Say Yes* to Jim?" With multiple urgent
projects to be finished, an annual multi-day marketing seminar for
business owners from all around the world just days away, and a
massive flurry of last-minute activities before taking a nearly
month-long European vacation, I certainly don't have the time for
this! (I even regretted it, but as this book reminded me, "regret is
just a progress killer," so I stopped.) Then I remembered why Jim

Palmer asked me to introduce you to his sixth book: Because I'm no stranger to just saying YES!

From leaving my parent's home and fending for myself at 14... To moving to a different continent and immigrating to the USA (without speaking English, zero connections, only a high school diploma, and with just $194) at 18... To saying yes to opportunities to take on jobs I had no idea how to do, which later became the keystones to my success... To doing whatever it took and turning that $194 into my first million-dollar business... To saying yes to scary financial investments – buying, growing, and selling businesses... To – most importantly – saying YES to becoming the person I am today... I think in his request, Jim believed I could impress upon you that without saying YES to opportunities in front of you, not much growth happens. And the first YES I want you to say right now is to invest in this book.

Why pick up this book? Because life as an entrepreneur is not all "rainbows and kittens." Anyone who promises you an easy, overnight success is likely angling for that remaining spending limit on your credit cards and telling you only what you want to hear. Because the reality is that being an entrepreneur and building your own business is not for the pansies.

You'll get scared. You'll get frustrated. Some of your worst "what ifs" will come true. You'll need to make decisions without having enough information. You'll have to take on jobs you don't know how to do. You'll have to tackle opportunities that scare the lights out of you, and move forward even when you feel you don't have enough time, resources, and know-how to do so! But that's okay. Because in the following pages, you'll discover how to develop an ability to address and overcome whatever challenges come your way. This book will increase your capacity to *Just Say Yes* to trust in your own ability to figure things out.

In Chapter One, Jim will inspire you with his journey. In Chapter Three, he'll give hope and courage. In Chapter Four, you'll discover that "I can't" is not your problem. In Chapter Five,

Jim will take away all your excuses. In Chapter Seven, you'll get clear on your definition of a Dream Business. In Chapter Eight, you'll discover a "million-dollar platform" formula and read stories of overcoming nearly impossible-to-beat odds that will get you so fired up you'll have to restrain yourself to not bolt into immediate action and keep reading the next chapter. Chapter Nine will show you a way to exponentially increase your capacity to receive the abundance of everything you desire. In short, if "Bigger, Bolder, Faster" is what you're after in your life and business, *Just Say Yes* is for you!

And Jim Palmer is just the guy to learn this from. When I first met him nearly a decade and a half ago, the man was the king of "small ball." (You'll learn about it in Chapter Four.) Mired in busy work, even a mention of the word "mindset" would trigger him to spew a barrage of comments of what he really thought of "this new age-y, So-Cal-green-smoothie-drinking-hippie mumbo-jumbo BS"! But in that decade and half, I watched Jim challenge himself to *Just Say Yes* to bigger and bolder dreams and to achieve them ever faster and with a greater ease! I watched him transform himself from buying into his "head trash" to mastering his "head-game." From a guy has who at 50 hasn't even ventured out for Thai food (true story) to now live adventurously and run his Dream Businesses aboard his "Floating Home"... that's why when it comes to knowing something about increasing the capacity to *Just Say Yes*, Jim is your man!

Which brings me back to my first words and the third reason I discovered why so many people fail to achieve their dreams (you probably thought I forgot it, didn't you?).

It's inaction! In Chapter Three, Jim takes a look at some of the opportunities he said yes to. But there is one thing he left out – likely because it would make this book too long to read – the time and effort he put in each and every time to back up his decision.

Please note: If you're looking for a magic "quick-fix" formula, you won't find it here. In my experience, there's no such thing. It takes real commitment to transform what is into what can be. That's why more than 90 percent of people who attend short seminars see no improvement in their lives. They don't act on what they learn. If you want to build your Dream Business, you must say yes to doing the work!

So, I challenge you to recognize the opportunity that's in your hands. Don't just read this book; act on it. Don't let *Just Say Yes* become another buzzword you read in a book or shouted at a seminar. Use the lessons to reinvent yourself and your business. Choose to become a *Just Say Yes* entrepreneur and transform your life, your business, and the lives of people you serve.

Whatever your big, bold, urgent dream is, make it bigger, bolder, and go for it faster because you now have the map for turning dreams into reality in your hands.

Go ahead – *Just Say Yes*… I believe in you!

Adam Urbanski
Millionaire Marketing Mentor
www.TheMarketingMentors.com

Acknowledgements

On a cold January morning, this book was literally God-inspired, as you'll read in Chapter One. But long before that cold morning, God saved my life 16 years ago. After facing what I describe as my "season of crisis" – 15 months of devastating unemployment, debt, shattered confidence, and just for good measure, Stage II cancer – God rescued me, inspired me to become an entrepreneur, and my life has been simply extraordinary and blessed ever since.

A big thank you to Stephanie, my wife of 37 years, my greatest supporter, best friend, and now partner. She is an amazingly patient person and, more than anyone, has taught me the importance of serving others. It was also Stephanie's idea to go on a "big adventure," and that led to our becoming "live aboards" and cruising the waters of the east coast of the United States.

My four children, Nick, Steve, Jessica, and Amanda are all doing well on their own, and both Jessica and Amanda have blessed us with grandchildren! But even from a distance, they continue to cheer me on, and I could not be prouder of the adults they have become.

The amazing growth of my business would not be possible without my incredible support team – my Dream Team! Thank you to my remarkable personal assistant, client service manager and friend, Kate; the Sensei of my web presence, Adam; my lead designer, Chris; my interview scheduler, Stephanie; amazing client support rep and Concierge lead designer, Lyndsay, for providing outstanding client support to our hundreds of valued clients; Amy for the hundreds of "Dream Business" graphics that make me look so good; Julie-Ann, Helen, and Matt for leading my team of content writers; Mike and his team at Mikel Mailings; Bobby and the entire team at Synapse for being outstanding partners in my Concierge Print and Mail on Demand program; and thank you to Ann Deiterich for doing a wonderful job editing this book. Ann has been a part of all my books, and she's done an incredible job taking both my written words and my thoughts and making me sound a lot smarter than I am!

Today, Stephanie and I get to literally live our dream lifestyle on our boat, Floating Home. I coach entrepreneurs and small business owners, and do about 140 interviews a year, all working three days a week as we see some of the most beautiful land (and water) that this country has to offer.

Thank you to all of my clients who entrust me to help them build their Dream Businesses. I can't imagine a more fun and rewarding life – but I'm always open to new ideas!

I want to thank you – the reader of this book. Writing a book, let alone seven books, is a daunting task. And if it were not for the countless notes, emails, and reviews, I might not have made it past the first book. I hope that in some way, as I share some of my story, you too will be inspired to *Just Say Yes* and live your dream lifestyle.

Finally, I want to thank Dan Kennedy, my greatest business mentor. I read my first Dan Kennedy book back in 2006, and it resonated so much with his entrepreneurial instincts and savvy marketing strategies that I ordered his entire library at the time. One of my greatest moments as an entrepreneur was when Dan Kennedy said this about my book, *DECIDE*:

"Jim Palmer is a consummate entrepreneur, particularly adept at getting people focused on creating their 'Dream Business' not just any successful business. His book, *DECIDE. The Ultimate Success Trigger,* synthesizes important distinctions in business and personal behavior, in simple, actionable terms."

To Your Success,

Chapter One: My Journey – Your Blueprint

I'm glad you just said yes to picking up this book. I understand that as a busy entrepreneur, you only have so much time, and besides looking for a return on every dollar you invest, you're also concerned about finding an ROI on your investments of time. I share quite a bit about my journey as an entrepreneur and I do so solely because I believe my story can serve as a blueprint to expedite your own path to success.

In this first chapter, I want to give you a better foundation and greater understanding of where I've been and where I'm coming from, **so you can fully digest the information that I'm about to share**. I'll *try* to be brief... or at least as brief as I can be.

I write this, my seventh business book, presuming you've read at least one or two of my previous works... at least that's what my ego is hoping! But if this is the first book of mine that you're reading, prepare yourself for something unique or at least different than most other business books.

My first three books (*The Magic of Newsletter Marketing, Stick Like Glue,* and *The Fastest Way to Higher Profits*) were part of a well thought out positioning strategy as my career as an entrepreneur was blossoming. Book four (*It's Okay to Be Scared*) was somewhat of a labor of love with my friend and fellow cancer survivor, Martin Howey.

For most authors, especially busy entrepreneurs, writing a book is all-consuming, and while being an author helps you build authority and perceived status, in most cases, it is just a bridge too far for many – but I digress.

After writing my first four books, I decided to take a break from writing and focus on other ways to grow my various businesses. Then, about year after making this decision, I was inspired … to write another book! My fifth book came as more of an idea or actually a response to a question I kept getting from coaching clients, potential coaching clients, and from people who were interviewing me. While the question was sometimes framed slightly differently, it was essentially, "What's the best time to start a business or when is the best time to grow or expand my current business?" In all cases, my answer was the same: *Stop Waiting for*

It to Get Easier! That phrase – a mantra, really – became the title of book five. I was proud of that book for a number of reasons, not the least of which was having original *Shark Tank* investor, Kevin Harrington, write the foreword. As I said, I was inspired to write book five, and I'm thankful I just said yes.

Stop Waiting did very well, and having Kevin Harrington write the foreword felt like the crème de la crème for me as both an author and entrepreneur, and once again, I unofficially put away my keyboard, satisfied with becoming a five-time author, all while running a rapidly growing business.

And then it happened again, dang it! I was again inspired to write another book and am I ever glad I just said yes.

In 2013, I created the Dream Business Academy (DBA), a unique three-day live event during which I teach entrepreneurs and small business owners how to grow their own Dream Businesses, so they too can live their dream lifestyles. At my first event in Las Vegas, I shared for about an hour some of the most personal and intimate details of my life as a business owner – kind of the "good, the bad and the ugly." I mean, I really went out on a limb and pulled back the curtain.

As I was sharing some of the hard lessons about being in debt, scared, and yet still having to invest more borrowed money to keep my dream alive, I saw a couple entrepreneurs in the audience with tears in their eyes. When some of the attendees at the first event shared how much they appreciated my candor, I decided to repeat this segment at the next event.

After a few DBAs, some of the attendees were starting to encourage me to share "this personal success and mindset stuff" with a larger audience... other than the people attending my live events. In reality, they were telling me to write my next book. Did I want to write another book? Not really, but I saw this as an opportunity to help more people overcome some of their own fears and personal demons that were most likely inhibiting their personal growth and the growth of their businesses. So without a really solid plan, I once again decided to *Just Say Yes* and started writing what would be my most important book to date – *DECIDE: The Ultimate Success Trigger.*

After six books and an audio book entitled *Serve First*, I decided that once and for all my authoring days were over. You'd think I'd learn to stop saying that!

I had six books, the covers of which fit nicely into two frames behind my desk, important when you do as many interviews as I do. So, life is good, check the box on becoming an author, and perhaps start sleeping past 4:30 a.m.

And then it happened again. Inspiration, and this time the messenger was unmistakable.

This time I was inspired while walking my rescue dog, Blue, early one morning on the farm where my wife, Stephanie, and I were renting a small cottage. And this time I was nudged by the Holy Spirit. I heard in my heart the message, "Bigger, Bolder, Faster." When I heard that message, we were about four weeks

11

away from my Dream Business Academy event in Orlando, and my brain was in perpetual business mode.

So when I heard "Bigger, Bolder Faster," I smiled and said, "Yes, I like that message. I will teach 'Bigger, Bolder, Faster' in Orlando at Dream Business Academy!"

Then I received another signal that was unmistakably directed right at me: "You too, Jim – for 2017, you too go bigger, bolder, and faster. You step up *your own* game! And, I want you to get this message out to a larger audience than simply those entrepreneurs who watch your weekly videos or come to your live events. Make *Bigger, Bolder Faster* your next book!"

The little voice in my head was saying, "No, I don't want to write another book!"

"*Just Say Yes*, Jim – do it!"

When I heard, "*Just Say Yes*," I knew that had to be the overarching message of the book, with "Bigger, Bolder, Faster" as a part of it. On that cold morning, I felt that every entrepreneur and small business owner has within them the desire, and perhaps ability, to play a bigger, bolder and faster game. I felt that way two months ago, and I still feel it today. And more importantly, it is my greatest desire that if you are not yet achieving your dreams and goals as an entrepreneur, that this book will prove to be the inspiration you need to – *Just Say Yes* and go bigger, bolder and faster!

Just Say Yes… to an Adventure

If you have not followed me on social media or regularly watched my videos, you may be wondering, "Farm? Cottage? Renting?" Let me catch you up because how that occurred is a big part of my decision to *Just Say Yes* and take the leap to live my own dream lifestyle.

In June 2016, Stephanie retired from a 15-year career in early childhood development. She has dedicated a large part of her life to children, and honestly, she was feeling burned out from the enormous responsibility and wanted to take some time to figure out what would be next for her.

One day, before she retired, Stephanie came home after work and said, "I think it's time for an adventure." I smiled and asked her what she had in mind. She said she didn't know the "what" but felt that we'd lived most of our lives safely and "by the book," and now it was time to do something different for an adventure. "We've raised our four kids, we greatly enjoy time with our three beautiful grandchildren, and now as empty-nesters, we should do something fun and adventurous. We are blessed with good health and are still young (that's relative)." Okay, sign me up!

Stephanie was about to retire from her successful career in child care to work part time for my coaching business, and since I can do my work – coaching entrepreneurs and small business owners – anywhere as long as I have internet and a phone connection, we were no longer geographically tied to any one place. We binge watched HGTV and the many shows about beach living and island hopping, and we began to research living in the Caribbean for a year until one day Stephanie suggested, "What about living on a boat?" Again, sign me up!

Three years ago, we bought a 30' Sea Ray Cruiser and absolutely fell in love with boating and the incredible stress-relieving aspects of being on the water. That boat, Perfect Timing, was a great weekend boat but too small to live aboard full time, so we began the journey of looking for our next perfect boat... the one that would become our floating home!

Long story short: We found the most perfect boat that would feel like "a home on the water" at the Annapolis Power Boat Show in October 2016. The only problem was that it was out of our price range, but we sure loved that boat! Stephanie snapped this picture of me standing in the boat with "my wheels turning,"

 desperately trying to think of a way to buy this boat, without taking on another big mortgage!

Driving home from the boat show, we both came back to reality and settled back into our agreed-upon budget, so I began searching online for the same make and model boat, only a couple years older. Incredibly, I found one, and it was only two and a half hours away. Our soon-to-be new floating home is a 2006 Carver Motor Yacht. It's 50′ of pure "make-me-smile amazing" and we wanted it bad! But there was one small detail to address – we needed to sell our house.

Our beloved family home for the past 28.5 years was now going on the market. Yes after raising four children there, we have so many wonderful memories, which made it a little bittersweet, but we both felt that the time was right. It was time to *Just Say Yes* to our new big adventure. To maximize our funds, Stephanie and I agreed to try to sell the house ourselves for 60 days. If we were not successful, we agreed to then hire a real estate agent.

We hired a professional home stager and house photographer (both truly amazing investments), and after about a month's worth of packing, several big trips to Goodwill, and putting some of our furniture and personal possessions in storage, we were finally ready to list the house. As daunting as selling a house seemed at first, we spent some time doing research and contemplating the steps along the way, and in the end, when we considered how much money we could save, we just said yes and decided to act as our own agent!

I figured out how to get our house on MLS and all of the popular homes-for-sale websites and within 12 hours of our listing going live, our phone started to ring! We showed the house ten times in the first three days and received an offer that first weekend! Given the heavy traffic, we decided to turn down the offer and keep going for full price or close to it. In the end, we sold the house ourselves in five weeks for a price we were very happy with.

House sold – now make offer on our dream boat!

The owner of the boat accepted our offer, and we set the wheels in motion to beat the fast-approaching cold winter season when most boats are pulled from the water and stored on land. Our goal was to settle on the house and buy the new boat in time to drive it three and a half hours north to Chesapeake City, Maryland (our hailing port) and winterize it there. This would make it closer to home, so we could visit it often and prepare it more easily for our spring departure. This is a screenshot from a boating app which shows our initial voyage on December 8th from Deale, Maryland, just south of Annapolis north to Chesapeake City, Maryland.

House sold, boat purchased; now we needed a place to live for five months!

We needed to find a short-term furnished month-to-month rental that would allow us bring our 75-pound dog, Blue, with us – no small task! Yes, Blue will be joining us on the boat, and our cat, Serendipity, is now living with our son, Steve. Stephanie took care of the task of finding us a place to live, and she found us a great little hideaway – a one-bedroom cottage on a local farm. And bonus: it's 20 minutes closer to the marina.

We Just Said Yes, So What's the Plan?

Having said yes to this big adventure, Stephanie and I have agreed to an 18-month plan. Starting in the spring, on or about

May 1st or sooner, we'll leave land and, together with Blue, cruise to Rhode Island. We rented a slip at a marina close to one of our daughters and two grand kids. It will be a fun summer!

In October, we'll begin cruising south on the Intracoastal Waterway (ICW) to Florida for the winter. That's right, no more snow – I have shoveled my last driveway! In spring 2018, we'll cruise back north to our hailing port in Chesapeake City, Maryland and spend the summer there on the beautiful Chesapeake Bay.

We haven't agreed to what happens after that, but we've both been reading a lot of books about people who live aboard boats and cruise the Great Loop. The Great Loop is the continuous waterway that encompasses the eastern portion of North America, including the Atlantic and Gulf Intracoastal Waterways, the Great Lakes, the Canadian Heritage Canals, and the inland rivers of America's heartland. That might be our next big adventure but no firm plans yet.

One thing Stephanie and I have learned in this process, even before we shove off from the dock, is that life is truly an adventure and sometimes you don't know what the next day will bring in terms of both opportunity and challenge. But you wake up every day, *Just Say Yes*, and figure it out!

This new adventure is a little outside our comfort zone, but we are both so excited and happy that we said yes to doing something other than what is typically described as normal and safe.

One last thing, naming the new boat – no easy task! After much thought and debate with family over Thanksgiving dinner, we've named our dream boat, Floating Home!

Many of our family and friends are curious about the how, what, where, and why we're doing this. That's a big reason that Stephanie and I decided to start a blog about our adventure. We've loved sharing the Perfect Timing with friends and family for the last three years, and now the blog will let us share some of our Floating Home adventures. (If you're interested in following along, we're going to be documenting much of our adventure at www.OurFloatingHome.com.)

We have a lot more learning to do and many more things to consider as life is about to get very different. But we are super excited about figuring it out and doing this big crazy adventure together.

Fun Fact: When Stephanie first proposed doing some big adventure, we of course were thinking of the many reasons doing something like this might not be the safe or prudent thing to do. And the very next morning, she received one of those inspirational emails containing this quote from Hunter S. Thompson:

"Life should not be a journey to the grave with the intention of arriving safely in a pretty and well-preserved body, but rather to skid in broadside in a cloud of smoke, thoroughly used up, totally worn out, and loudly proclaiming,

'Wow! What a ride!'"

We both knew that was God's way of saying, ***"Just say yes!"***

Why My Plan Matters to You

So, now that you're caught up – back to the cold morning on the farm walking with Blue.

When I felt the inspiration (and nudging) to ***Just Say Yes*** and write this book, my mind opened widely, and I began to think about how many good things in my life have happened as a result of me just saying yes, even when I felt I wasn't ready... or even when I felt very scared and uncertain, when I felt like I should stick to "safe and prudent" instead.

I'm choosing to share my story because I know that I am not special. In fact, I know that I'm just a pretty regular guy. My inspiration to write this book is not to gloat about the success that I've been blessed with, nor is it my intention to boast about being able to *Just Say Yes* to living my dream lifestyle. (And I fully appreciate that my dream lifestyle of living on a boat may well be a far cry from yours!)

The point is that if I can do this and achieve what I have, then so can you. Think about your own dream lifestyle for a moment. What do you want to do every day? Where do you want to live? How do you want to spend your time… and with whom? I'm living proof that just by saying yes, you will put yourself on the path to achieve your own Dream Business and dream lifestyle.

Will it be easy? No. You have to put in the effort; however, simply working hard is not the answer. You have to be alert to all the forks in the road you're traveling on and *Just Say Yes* when opportunities present themselves, no matter how scared you might be. You have to *Just Say Yes* rather than sticking to the safe, predictable, or prudent thing to do. I share my story as an example to help you uncover for yourself the opportunities to which you should *Just Say Yes*, no matter how scary they may seem at the time.

While I thought that I'd use the theme "Bigger, Bolder, Faster" at my Dream Business Academy – Orlando, the theme quickly became *"Just Say Yes"* instead with attendees starting to chant that mantra several times during our three days together. In fact, at the conclusion of the event, one attendee approached and said, "When I arrived to register and saw the table with your books for sale, I thought, 'Great. Another business guru who just wants to sell his stuff.' But by lunch on day one, I realized that you were a regular guy who was sharing his success story… and it was one that I could replicate as long as I learned to *Just Say Yes*!"

That comment made me realize that it's a powerful message that I want to share, and this book is the best way to do that. I'm asking you to suspend your normal belief system about what might be normal – or safe and prudent – and open your mind as you read this book to how just saying yes can and will change your life. First, decide that you want to create your Dream Business and live your own dream lifestyle, and then, whatever it takes to make that dream a reality, *Just Say Yes*!

Chapter Two:
Two "F" Words: Fear and
Forgiveness

It can be a scary thing to *Just Say Yes.* There is no shortage of situations that can instill fear, and there is also very likely no shortage of mistakes you've already made throughout your life. I have two "F" words that are very important for you to embrace: fear and forgiveness.

As an entrepreneur and no matter where you might be on your entrepreneurial path toward success, I'm willing to bet that you've had what I call the "3:00 a.m. holy crap" moment.

It's when you're lying in bed, awake in the middle of the night, wondering how you are going to make payroll or pay the bills, thinking that you haven't paid yourself in six months, and wondering how much longer you can keep going. Should you tap more of your savings or increase the amount you put on your credit card? Maybe borrow from someone you know or a family member? You believe in your dream and you know you want to continue, but you feel stuck.

If you aren't achieving what you want, I can guarantee it is not because you lack the skill or the desire. It's because you are holding yourself back, staying in your own comfort zone, and not doing what you need to do in order to be successful.

So when you have your next "3:00 a.m. holy crap" moment, get up, walk to the bathroom, turn on the light, and look into the mirror. Ask the person looking back at you why that person is holding you back. Demand accountability from that person. In no uncertain terms, ask, "Why are you doing this to me? Why don't you want me to succeed?"

r too many entrepreneurs are the impediment to their ess. If we were to examine any of the tens of thousands of es that have failed, the common cause would be that the business owner continued to lie in bed staring at the ceiling at 3:00 a.m., doing nothing more than worrying.

Yes, I certainly had my own "3:00 a.m. holy crap" moment, and I decided that slow-to-no growth was no longer acceptable and I demanded accountability from the guy in the bathroom mirror. For some, the "3:00 a.m. holy crap" moment is one in which the business owner asks, "If not now, when?" And "someday" is a really lousy answer because, if you aren't already aware of it, "someday" never arrives.

Forgive Yourself

I want you to hold yourself accountable, but I also want you to forgive yourself for past mistakes. Probably the only thing worse than making mistakes is *not* making any mistakes. If you aren't making any mistakes, it indicates that you really aren't doing anything. Mistakes do not deter forward progress; inaction does!

Just Say Yes!

Let go of regret and forgive yourself or you will never make progress toward what it is you want to achieve.

Regret is another progress killer. I've learned in working with my coaching clients that what holds them back is the negativity or remorse they feel over past mistakes. I hear comments like, "I tried that a few years ago and it didn't work. I invested in that and it didn't pay off." I'll get a litany of mistakes that they made that has caused them to fear trying again. Even worse, those mistakes have generated regrets. When you live with regret, it's a progress killer.

Your brain can only process one thought at a time. If you're thinking about something negative, there is no room to think about something positive. You have to shut down the negativity. You have to forgive yourself for past mistakes. Perhaps you didn't jump when you had the chance and missed the boat; perhaps you didn't invest when the opportunity was in front of you; or maybe you were just plain scared. Forgive yourself. You can't undo those mistakes and you can't create a new beginning, but you can learn from your past and create a new ending.

No more woulda, coulda, shoulda! Tell yourself, "Hey self. Congratulations. I'm not as bad as I thought. I'm going to forgive myself and start fresh right now!"

Make Forgiveness Real

If you're harboring ill feelings or unable to move forward due to some lingering resentment, forgiving someone else, or even yourself, can be done quiet effectively by making and doing something physical. There are different variations of this, but essentially you want to write down the "it" on a piece of paper or index card. The "it" is whatever the thing is that you can't seem to forgive – what someone did or said to you, one of your own failures, etc.

With it in tangible form, you'll now get rid of it by burning it in the fireplace, tearing it to pieces and stepping on it, or even burying it in the backyard. Whichever disposal option you choose (or create one of your own), as you rid yourself of this burden, say a few words such as "I am no longer going to think about this or let it weigh me down. From this moment forward, this will be nothing more than a distant memory and bump in the road. I choose to let go and move forward."

Be sure to say this aloud and not simply in your head. If you're so inclined, you can also pray about this as you release it, but either way, the physical act of destroying it and taking a positive forward step to move past it will do wonders.

23

Mindset Is a Terrible Thing to Waste

Years ago, there was an advertisement for education that included the tagline, "A mind is a terrible thing to waste." I believe the same thing is true about your mindset. If your mindset is negative, it is causing you to waste time and to fail. Not only is a mindset a terrible thing to waste, it's incredibly powerful.

Anything is possible when you *Just Say Yes*. Conversely, even the simplest thing may seem impossible when you are conditioned to believe that to be true.

If you're unsure as to the utter power of the mind, consider this perfect illustration in the story of an elephant. An African elephant is one of the strongest creatures on the planet. It can tip over automobiles and even railroad cars... right off the track. The elephant is so strong it can grasp a tree with its trunk and pull it out of the ground, root ball and all. It is powerful beyond limits.

However, now consider the alternative. An elephant born in captivity had a chain placed on its ankle when it was very young. The chain was attached to a simple stake in the ground. The baby elephant would walk as far as the chain would reach in one direction, and then be stopped. So it would change direction and repeat the process, stopping when the chain had reached its length. This baby elephant was conditioned to believe that he could only walk so far in any one direction, but no farther. He could look around and see the trees, water, and perhaps the other elephants roaming free, but he could not move beyond the length of the chain. As he grew, even becoming an adult, he certainly had the strength a hundred times over to pull that stake out of the ground and walk wherever he wanted. The elephant born into captivity with a chain around its ankle had the strength... perhaps even the desire. Yes, he certainly had both, however, because his brain told him he couldn't do it, he never pulled that simple stake from the ground to go where he wanted. His mindset had been conditioned throughout his young life to cause him to believe that little stake limited and dictated his movement.

As an entrepreneur, your brain works the same way. Like the baby elephant that doesn't believe he can pull that stake out of the ground and walk anywhere he wants to, it probably hasn't occurred to you to try what you have been conditioned to believe is impossible.

I have yet to meet an entrepreneur or small business owner who doesn't have some sort of chain around his or her leg. Even highly successful entrepreneurs have something, a thought or belief, that is preventing them from moving forward and achieving even more success. Think about what shackles have been holding you back. The next time you're alone quietly with your own thoughts, be honest with yourself about it: What is the limiting belief you have been suppressing and simply finding "work arounds" for most of your career? What would your business and life look like if you were able to change your mindset and *Just Say Yes* to doing whatever it is you have not been able to do – thus far? What is it that you really want to achieve? What is your own dream lifestyle? If you're tired of slow-to-no growth, if you're tired of just getting by or living week to week, if you're tired being tired and watching the sand run out of the hour glass – then take the step to get the help you need. Break the chain and bust out. *Just Say Yes* to doing what it is you want to do! You deserve all the success you can create for yourself. Period and amen.

Just Say Yes to Taking Out the Trash!

The baby elephant is a victim of his own head trash – limiting beliefs about what is or isn't possible. Head trash is the negative stuff floating around in your brain. We all have head trash, and it's time to *Just Say Yes* to getting rid of it. It stinks, and it's time to kick it to the curb. It's very real, and it can be a real crippler or even a killer to your efforts and your business.

Head trash is comprised of an enormous collection of feelings, thoughts, beliefs, and experiences that have been piling up since childhood. Your head trash is constantly reinforcing what you can't achieve. It's the ankle shackle that is holding you back when, in reality, you have all the strength and skill you need to achieve great things.

I certainly had my own head trash and limiting beliefs about what I couldn't do, including speaking to large groups, creating videos, writing books, launching a podcast, and hosting my own live events. I decided to stop being the impediment to my own success, and that meant I had to *Just Say Yes* to getting rid of the head trash, negative thoughts, and worry that seemed to continually swirl in my brain, often at 3:00 a.m.

Every entrepreneur has head trash that they have to overcome. How much time do you spend worrying about the "what ifs"? All of the effort and energy that goes into worry and fear generates nothing but negativity, and that negativity becomes stifling. It's stopping your progress. And it's self-inflicted. It's time to *Just Say Yes* to looking in the mirror and holding the person looking back accountable. Understand that the person in the mirror has the capacity to take out the trash! Swirling negative thoughts create negative actions that become negative patterns and habits. Think anything good, let alone great, can evolve from that? Absolutely not!

Head trash has its foundation in fear. Inspirational speaker, the late, great Zig Ziglar had this to say about fear: "F-E-A-R has two meanings: 'Forget Everything and Run' or 'Face Everything and Rise.' The choice is yours."

Which will you choose? If you want to create a Dream Business and live your dream lifestyle, it's time to take out the head trash and kick fear to the curb. It's time to *Just Say Yes* and face everything and rise instead.

Criticism is another contributor to head trash, and it's everywhere. If you really want to be successful, you are going to have to become immune to criticism! Failure to do so means that your head trash will continue to pile up and pile up. It will become a stinking mess. You'll end up spending all of your time trying to overcome negative thoughts and will be constantly taking out the trash instead of growing your business and profits.

Very simply, the only folks you need to please are your paying customers, and what they have to say is really the only thing you should be listening to in the first place. Most of the other criticism you will hear does nothing for your business. I believe some entrepreneurs let criticism cloud their judgments, and worse, alter the way they do business. They're afraid of what others think of them and are also afraid of failure. They're afraid to jump and learn to fly on the way down.

Like criticism, there is no shortage of opinions. Let me tell you something: There's only one opinion in the world that counts when it comes to running your business – your customer's… your **paying** customer's. Those people who are giving you money are the only ones who truly count. What they say matters, and that's what you should be listening to.

Very often, our peers, our friends, our families, business associates, and the people we hang out with will share their opinions. These people probably don't understand how to run a business and how to market a business unless they're entrepreneurs themselves. They don't understand how and why you make the decisions you do, but that doesn't stop them from sharing their opinions about what you do or how you're going about doing it.

Don't let their opinions contribute to your own head trash. *Just Say Yes* to becoming immune to criticism and ignoring the opinions of those people who are not contributing to your growth or your bottom line!

Since you only have room in your brain for one type of thought, make certain your thoughts are positive ones. Consider what *Shark Tank's* Daymond John has to say on the matter: "I believe the last thing I read at night will likely manifest when I'm sleeping. You become what you think about the most."

Affirmative Action Steps:

- ❖ *Every entrepreneur will have a "3:00 a.m. holy crap" moment. When it happens, hold the person in the mirror accountable.*
- ❖ *Decide not to be the impediment to you own success.*
- ❖ *Forgive yourself. Regret is a progress killer.*
- ❖ *Don't waste your mindset on the negative. Don't fill your head with self-limiting thoughts. Don't be like the baby elephant in the ankle shackle.*
- ❖ *Head trash is the accumulation of thoughts, feelings, beliefs, and experiences about what may or may not be possible. For most of us, it's negative. **Just Say Yes** to taking out your own head trash.*

❖ *When it comes to fear, decide that you are going to "Face Everything and Rise"!*

❖ *Be immune to criticism. It's a huge contributor to your head trash. The only opinion that matters is that of your paying customers.*

Chapter Three:
Success Leaves Tracks

When I started my journey as an entrepreneur in October 2001, I did a lot of reading and research, and one of my favorite authors was (and is) business legend, Dan Kennedy who is an expert marketer and very successful entrepreneur. One of the things he wrote that had a big impact on me was that "success leaves tracks."

That concept was good news for me when I was launching my first business, and it's good news for you now. Why? The "success leaves tracks" principle means that you don't have to reinvent the wheel. You have an example, or many examples, to follow. You can achieve success by taking the same steps and following in the footprints of other entrepreneurs who have already made it… and made it big in some cases. Their success tracks can be your personal road map to creating your own Dream Business!

However, having the map is not enough. You have to take the steps and those steps may be difficult at times, and every time you come to a fork in the road, you're going to have to *Just Say Yes*… no matter how frightening the unknown path in front of you might be. In many respects, you're going to have to jump and sprout your wings on the way down. Scary? You bet. Are you going to hit bottom? You might, but if that happens, you pick yourself up, dust yourself off, figure out what didn't work, and try again.

I know the idea of hitting bottom is scary, but the alternative is staying put with your feet firmly on solid ground, accepting the fact that you'll never know if you can fly, you'll never discover everything that you can achieve, and you'll never be able to create your Dream Business and live the lifestyle you want.

31

There's also another way to look at this: Perhaps you are already at the bottom, stuck in a job in which you're simply trading hours for dollars or facing unemployment or underemployment. That's exactly where I was when I decided to launch my business, and although I had no money and a lot of debt, I just said yes and took the leap.

Forks in the Road

In looking back over my life, there were plenty of forks in the road on my entire career journey and plenty of times I just said yes that played a large role in getting me to where I am today.

Let me share a few of the times I just said yes with you. After reading this chapter, I encourage you to do this same exercise. Take some time to consider the journey you've already been on. Reflect on the many times you've already just said yes, perhaps without realizing it at the time. My guess is that your life is filled with examples, similar to mine, that got you to where you are today. Having coached entrepreneurs to higher levels of success for more than seven years, I can tell you that we all are occasionally too hard on ourselves. And recognizing successes, no matter how small, is a great way to boost your self-confidence – perhaps just enough to take the next leap!

When I was 15, I was offered a job as a bike mechanic at a local business within walking distance to where I went to high school. I had never worked on a bike in my life, and it would have been easy to use my lack of knowledge as the right reason to turn down the offer and perhaps find something else I could do to earn some spending money, but I said yes, and that decision led to a 25-year career in the bicycle industry.

At 21, I was offered the opportunity to manage a bike shop that the owner was planning to sell while he returned to his former career as an engineer. The business had low sales due in part to the terrible economy that surrounded the Carter-era recession. I'd never managed anything before, let alone a team, and certainly it was a lousy economic environment in which to prove myself. I was just about to get married and was looking for something more career oriented, and again, it would have been easy – perhaps even prudent – to walk away from that opportunity to look for something else with greater growth potential. But I just said yes, and I ended up growing that business from approximately $300K in sales to just shy of $1 million dollars, catching the eye of a local competitor.

This competitor had a small chain of 14 bike stores and offered me a regional manager's position but also wanted my help with marketing. I never finished college and only had one marketing class, but I did some creative marketing at the previous bike shop – including starting a newsletter – so I just said yes and kept moving forward, believing that I would somehow figure it out or at least look good trying my best!

A year later, the owner said he was going to start franchising his business and needed someone to develop a franchise training program for new franchise owners. "We will need to create a training manual and develop a two-week training program to teach new franchisees the bike business." I'd never created a training program in my life, let alone be responsible for helping someone who made a personal investment of $150K know how to run a successful business, but once again I just said yes! I later went on to become the National Director of Franchise Operations, and we grew that chain of 14 stores to 80 stores in 18 states.

Just Say Yes! Like me, you've probably arrived at plenty of forks in the road.

After 10 years with this company, I was offered a position to help start a new marketing association in the retail musical instrument business. I had no clue how associations worked and other than being a self-taught hack musician, I had no experience to speak of in the music business – at least in my mind. Luckily, the three partners starting this business believed in me and the experience I had, and I just said yes! The owners had a super aggressive goal of achieving a membership base of $500 million in combined revenue in less than two years. I said yes, and together we hit that goal.

Exactly two years after we hit that goal, I was offered a position as VP of Marketing for a local training company. Again, no previous experience in this field (other than training new franchisees), but the salary they were offering was great and since I had personal career goal to become a VP by them time I was 40, you guessed it, I just said yes, knowing that I would figure it out later. I was going to jump and learn how to sprout wings.

Unfortunately, later never came because this "too good to be true" job offer was just that, and upon returning from a family vacation in July 2000, I was told that "my position was being eliminated." Bam, just like that – my steady job history since saying yes to becoming a bike mechanic at age 15 had come to an end.

I'll spare you the details here, but what I believed would be a short-lived period of unemployment followed by me receiving multiple lucrative job offers turned into 15 months of devastating unemployment. To make matters worse and even more stressful, one year into this difficult journey of unemployment, I was diagnosed with stage II cancer.

Since I promised to spare you the details, let me cut to the chase about what has to be the "granddaddy" of all my decisions to *Just Say Yes*.

At the lowest point in my life – out of work for 15 months, broke and heavily in debt, seeing any prospects for a job vanish with the terrorist attack of September 11, 2001, and having successfully attained cancer-free status (for now) but still badly shaken about having to face my own mortality and the thought of not seeing my twin girls graduate from high school – I got on my knees and prayed for divine intervention. I needed guidance, and I needed it desperately.

It was during this prayer for guidance that the Holy Spirit told me to start a business… to become an entrepreneur.

"Seriously? Do you have the right number? It's me, Jim Palmer…. I am broke and heavily in debt; my once strong ego, self-confidence, and self-esteem have been crushed; I don't know if I have the confidence or ability to sell anyone anything… and I'm supposed to start a business… now?"

"*Just Say Yes*, Jim."

Luckily, I did say yes and my journey as an entrepreneur began in October 2001.

The rest of the story, the business owner piece of the puzzle, is what comes next and is perhaps more exciting, but I felt some historical context was in order as we entrepreneurs are always so forward looking, seemingly always looking to the future and not assessing some of the important revelations we can learn about ourselves by taking a look backward.

As I began writing this book, I took time to look back and I could clearly see all the forks in the road and how my decision at each one to *Just Say Yes* without knowing the how, when, or where have ultimately led me to a very good life.

From the humble beginning of my business and my first year as completely "revenue-free," I've continued to keep my eyes and ears open for subsequent opportunities and times to *Just Say Yes*.

From starting my business by providing a handful of clients with newsletters (remember, with no experience whatsoever: I created my first newsletter when I was a young 21-year-old store manager!), I said yes to expanding that to offering Customer-Loving Content™ to reach a much broader client base. I said yes to creating done-for-you newsletter templates and then my Concierge Print and Mail program, alleviating that pain my clients faced and growing my business again. I never thought of myself as an author and writing a book seemed very daunting. However, the successful entrepreneurs I was studying and learning from (remember, success leaves tracks) said that becoming an author is important, so I said yes to writing my first book, *The Magic of Newsletter Marketing*. When this revolution called social media began to evolve, I said yes to expanding again, creating my second successful online business, No Hassle Social Media, to create content badly needed by time-starved entrepreneurs. I didn't know much if anything about it, but I jumped and figured it out on the way down.

As a somewhat still new entrepreneur, when I attended my first major marketing event, my thinking was that I wanted to get "just one thing" out of it or make just "one good contact." Sitting in the back of large room, I remember looking around at everyone there and wondered, "Who's really successful and who's just pretending to be successful? And that's me right now – I feel like I'm pretending!" I figured the folks on stage doing the presenting were successful, but I thought, "I'm not going to do that. I'm not good at speaking in front of a group, so I'm not going to stand up in front of 500 people.

"Write a book? Well despite the fact that I feel like I barely got out of high school English, I had managed that one.

"Do videos? I'm not comfortable in front of a camera.

"Produce my own seminars to be successful in the coaching business? That's way too expensive, and what if I suck at it?"

Continually, my ongoing thought when these ideas crossed my mind was "No way! That's not going to work for me. My business is different. I don't know how to do those things. It's going to be too expensive. I'm uncomfortable on camera and hate my voice."

However, thankfully I reached a point in my life and career as an entrepreneur where I was beyond tired of slow-to-no growth and the painfully slow growth was beginning to make me feel like a loser again. So I decided to fix that and ***Just Say Yes*** to everything that promised growth – as presented by highly successful entrepreneurs who I knew to be very successful doing exactly what it was they were preaching… but all those things were scary.

Again, I'm sharing my story because I know it is not unique and am willing to bet that you are seeing some of your own fears and trepidations in situations that parallel my journey. I assure

Just Say Yes!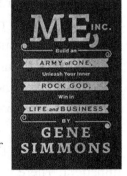

Tired of slow-to-no growth? *Just Say Yes* and expand your opportunities!

you, if you want to create your Dream Business and live your dream lifestyle, it's time to jump. It's time to *Just Say Yes*.

Me, Inc.

Maybe you've heard of Gene Simmons. Yes, that Gene Simmons – front man for the rock band, KISS. His full story is that of an entrepreneur more than simply a musician. He's a great example of someone who consistently just said yes, turning himself into a business conglomerate after starting out as a garage band. (Funny how so many successful ventures start in garages!)

After emigrating with his mother from Israel at age eight, he admits that his interest in starting a band had its foundation in watching the Beatles… or more specifically, watching the girls screaming at the Beatles. According to *Biography.com*, "He thought 'If I go start a band, maybe the girls will scream at me.' So, while attending Joseph Pulitzer Middle School, Simmons and a couple of friends created a band called The Missing Links in order to get the attention of their female classmates. The group, fronted by Simmons, won a school talent show, and gave Simmons a modicum of fame."

In his book, *Me, Inc. Build an Army of One, Unleash Your Inner Rock God, Win in*

Life and Business, Simmons shares that he and Paul Stanley always had a clear-cut vision of what they wanted to achieve and how they always planned to operate KISS as a business, not simply as a band. They decided to manage themselves (without a background in promotional management), began producing their own albums and marketing their licensed merchandise – again without formal training in any of these aspects of their business. Then came acting, including a few B-movies, as well as publishing and fashion plus a successful foray into reality television with *Gene Simmons Family Jewels.* Gene was the one who inspired me to reflect on my own journey – at all of the times I just said yes without feeling qualified or ready.

In his book, he shares his in-depth insights into business success, but – not to minimize his efforts, hard work and entrepreneurial talent – a lot of it boils down to deciding what you want and just saying yes, then figuring out how to go about achieving it and getting it. People who ***Just Say Yes*** are the ones who move forward, the ones who achieve success, the ones who live their own dreams, no matter how lofty those dreams may be.

A Little Tough Love

How you define success for yourself is completely up to you. Your success and dream lifestyle is probably not like mine and I'll also venture that it's not like that of Gene Simmons. (Or maybe the idea of wild makeup and screaming girls is right up your alley.) Regardless, I want you to dream big, decide, and ***Just Say Yes.*** But you must also be crystal clear in your understanding that you have to put in the work. No one hands it to you.

When I started as an entrepreneur, I knew in my heart and soul that I could be successful, but I figured I was going to do it my way. I ordered business cards – even opted for the more expensive glossy stock – and saw my name as "Founder and CEO." I thought I was doing well, but I got hungrier and more impatient. There were two game changers for me:

1) I learned to get comfortable doing uncomfortable things because it's the uncomfortable things that move you forward faster.
2) I also became involved with a mentor who kicked my butt and embarrassed me to create a turning point in my business.

I'll share that first embarrassing experience with being on the receiving end of some tough love in my entrepreneurial journey. I was part of a mastermind group when I was starting my own mastermind and coaching program. There were a lot of other successful coaches participating. At the time, my program was doing okay, but I wanted it to grow faster.

As I already mentioned, there were some things that I was not at all comfortable doing earlier in my career. As I was sharing with the group my desire to grow my business and listed a number of other entrepreneurs whom I admired and wanted to emulate (some of whom where in the room), a mentor, who was fully aware of what I was doing and *not doing*, got in my face – literally and figuratively – and said, "Jim, let me ask you a question. How is it that you feel that you deserve or are entitled to the same level of success as your peers and other people in the business if you aren't willing to do the same things that they're doing to grow their businesses? Explain that to me."

I now refer to this as my Rocky moment. Remember when Mr. T got in Rocky's face before the big fight. It had to be intimidating to say the least, but Rocky learned from that lesson, and I learned something about "manning up" and doing what is required to grow a Dream Business. I learned yet again from this embarrassing moment to put my fears aside and *Just Say Yes.*

It was painful and embarrassing. But… it was exactly the tough love I needed and what I needed pointed out to me. On the trip home, I made up my mind that, never again, would I be put in that position. Never again would I have my own "stuff" – my own shortcomings – put in my face like that. I had to own it.

When I say never again, I decided that never again was I going to be the impediment to my own success and growth. So I learned how to become a speaker; I learned how to create videos and put on my own live events. I became proficient at podcast interviews. I now have no trouble with doing any of those things that were once very, very uncomfortable to me. My discomfort level became a "too friggin' bad" perspective in my mind. I just said yes and figured them out because I saw other people having success by doing those things.

The people who achieve success are the people who do things that others are unwilling to do:
- **They make calls they'd rather not make.**
- **They get up earlier than they want to.**
- **They give more than they initially get in return.**
- **They're willing to feel unsure and insecure when playing it safe feels better.**
- **They deliver results instead of excuses.**
- **They're willing to fail and get up and try again.**
- **They always invest in themselves to accelerate their success.**

The top one percent are in the very small minority for a reason: Very few people are willing to do the hard things. That's exactly where I was before I put on my first live event. It was going to be very costly to book the room. Plus, I blocked a section of hotel rooms for better pricing for attendees, but I was going to be on the hook for those rooms even if no one showed up. I was very worried about that. I also worried about the room being packed and then choking and freezing on stage... forgetting everything I wanted to say. But I just said yes and got comfortable with this very uncomfortable approach.

How to get comfortable doing uncomfortable things:

1) Let go of your ego and your desire to create your own greatness. It didn't matter that I opted for the fancy stock on my business cards or that my title was "Founder and CEO." I finally realized that it is much less important that I'm the one who has every bright idea; it's much less important that I develop all the stuff I'm going to do. I learned that I can learn from someone else who's "been there, done that" and replicate that approach.

2) Seek help and counsel from really smart people and understand that you can actually purchase speed to grow your business. You can close the chasm between where you are right now and where you want to be and get there much faster.

3) Get a mentor. Yes, you'll be in for some tough love like I was in my embarrassing moment, but without accountability little actually gets done, and none of us is particularly good at holding ourselves accountable.

Yes, success leaves tracks, but you have to do things with which you might be very uncomfortable. Are you like I was? Feeling that you are entitled to the same level of success as others without getting over your own discomforts and doing what may be difficult at first? Too bad. Get over it. Yup, that's tough love, so figure out what you want and *Just Say Yes*.

Affirmative Action Steps:

❖ *While success does indeed leave tracks, you are the only one who can take the steps and **Just Say Yes** when you get to a fork in the road that leads to an unknown and perhaps scary path.*

❖ *Jump... and figure out how to sprout wings on the way down. Hitting bottom might seem scary, but, if you're like I was, you're already there... right now... at the bottom with no place to go but up.*

❖ *All entrepreneurs like to look forward and move full speed ahead. Writing this book forced me to look back at all the forks in the road I encountered and how saying yes has ultimately led me to where I am today.*

❖ *Gene Simmons is a great example of someone who continually just said yes to what he wanted and then figured out how to achieve it.*

❖ *People who **Just Say Yes** are the ones who move forward... the ones who succeed.*

❖ *You are going to have to get over any discomfort you feel about what you need to do to succeed. Your fears are simply "too friggin' bad." Get over it.*

❖ *The people who achieve success are the people who do things that others are unwilling to do.*

Chapter Four:
What If...?

You're probably second guessing or at least wondering about my advice that you should jump now and figure out how to sprout your wings as you fall. Clearly, it's not the safe or prudent thing to do.

But if you never jump, you'll never know if you can fly or to what heights you might soar.

In preparing for Stephanie's and my big adventure to live on a boat for at least 18 months, I recently read the book, *What's Up Ditch! The Ins and Outs of Cruising the Atlantic ICW: America's Secret Highway.* Ditch refers to the Intracostal Waterway which will be our route as we relocate from the north in the summer to Florida in the winter and back.

It's one of many books that my wife and I have read and researched to improve our chance of success in our venture. This research is akin to me "sprouting wings on the way down." We already jumped: we sold our house and bought the boat. Now we're learning as much as we can as fast as we can to avoid hitting the bottom.

If you've ever thought of doing something big, your mind probably plays the "what if" game. You might also get out a piece of paper or open a Word page to list all of the pros and cons about what you're considering. I've certainly been entrenched in plenty of what ifs about living on a boat and traveling the ICW:

- What if I run aground?
- What if I run out of gas?
- What if I hit another boat?
- What if I lose internet connection in the middle of a coaching call?

- What if this?
- What if that?
- What if, what if, what if?!?

I assure you, I have no shortage of what ifs going through my head. I mention the book *What's Up Ditch!* because the author, Chris DiCroce, specifically addressed almost all of the what ifs that were plaguing me.

Then he put a different spin on it: What if you do actually become a live aboard (the reference to those people who live on boats) and encounter some of the problems you're worried about and realize that you have the capacity to solve them and overcome them? Every day you wake up and tackle something else. As he put it, "What if you do this and discover that you're really a 'bad ass' and a really good boat captain and navigator?"

From the moment I read that passage in Chris's book, I never again doubted our decision to embark on this big adventure, and I also realized how many parallels there were for this "what if" game as it related to entrepreneurs.

Your Own Challenges

You are like me. I don't mean that you have decided to become a live aboard, but you've decided to pursue your entrepreneurial dream. At this point, you may have decided to jump and are currently in free fall trying to sprout wings. Or you might still be standing on the cliff staring at the bottom, worried about how far it is and what will happen if you fail to fly.

I know all of the what ifs that plague you with worry. I've had those same what ifs early in my career and at every fork in the road when I just said yes and chose the scary path.

What if I don't make any money? Whoa. I get that one. I referred to my first year in business as "revenue-free." It *was* scary. I had a family to support and was also thinking about college tuitions for my twins that were not going to be too far in the future. Yes, I used credit cards and changed my mindset to think of those as business loans rather than credit card debt. I persevered and kept networking and planting seeds that I had faith would germinate.

What if a client fires me? You pick yourself off, dust yourself and your ego off, and figure out why that happened. Was it your fault? Something you did wrong? If so, figure out the solution to avoid it from happening again. As for the client who fired you, can you remedy the solution to regain their trust?

Just Say Yes!

By protecting yourself from the occasional and limited sting of failure, you are actually deciding NOT to choose success. Fix that!

What if my new idea doesn't pan out? Again, you won't know until you try, but there are things you can do to test the waters beforehand. Do some sample marketing on a small scale as a litmus test. Confer with others in your industry or other entrepreneurs to get their take on your idea.

What if I lose the respect of my family and friends? Wouldn't you rather increase their respect by working hard to fulfill your dream? Honestly, unless your friends are entrepreneurs themselves, they probably aren't going to understand. They might be naysayers about your decision, but it's your life and your decision.

As it relates to the respect of your family and friends, for one thing, everyone respects success. People know it when they see it and most admire it. However, as it relates to the journey, your entrepreneurial goals and saying yes to doing some things outside of your comfort zone, know this: Your family and friends know you for who you are currently – not who you are moving and working to be. I encourage you not to seek their approval along the way because as much as they might love and support you, they might not understand some of the things you might be doing to increase your position in the marketplace and grow your business.

A quick example: My dad, who was a successful business man and someone for whom I have enormous respect, never understood why I would do speaking gigs, unpaid, and pay my own travel expenses! This was a foreign concept to him. Back in the day, you either got paid to speak or, at a minimum, had your travel costs reimbursed by the host. Had I not been so grounded in the belief that this strategy would ultimately help me build my business and the ROI would come later, based on me following the examples of highly successful entrepreneurs who already proved this strategy, I might have let my dad's opinion steer me off course. If you need support and encouragement along the way, join a mastermind group where like-minded people are also on the same journey. This will become your "other family" and the place for you to get support and encouragement.

Life Is a "What If"

So what if you do encounter these and other what ifs? If or when that happens, you get up every day, figure it out, apply the solution, and take the next step forward. When you take a much broader view, you'll see that all of life is actually one big "what if" game that you've been playing for years. Take a moment to think back on what you've faced so far in terms of the what ifs in your life:

- What if I don't make friends at the new school?
- What if I don't pass the driver's test?
- What if I don't have a prom date?
- What if I don't get into the college of my choice?
- What if I fail that class?
- What if I bomb the job interview?
- What if she doesn't say "yes"?

Sound familiar? You've probably dealt with all of those fears and "what if" worries... and plenty more! Yet here you are. Getting up every day, figuring it out, and moving forward.

Like the author of *What's Up Ditch*, let me now put a different spin on your "what if" fears about your entrepreneurial dream: What if it turns out you discover that you really are a "bad ass" entrepreneur and are great at growing your business? What if you have what it takes to create your Dream Business? What if you have the skill set and

Just Say Yes!
In reality, your entire life can be one big what if, so go for it and achieve what you want!

determination to be wildly successful? What if you figure out how to sprout wings when you jump and soar higher than you might have ever thought possible? What if you actually do move forward and build your Dream Business, making it possible for you to live your dream lifestyle?

Don't Say "Yes" to Small Ball!

You've no doubt heard that Rome wasn't built in a day. Very simply, big things are not accomplished in one day... or even one week or one month.

I know plenty of entrepreneurs who get stuck in short-term thinking and doing. They're in a continuous loop of getting out of bed every day and thinking, "What do I have to accomplish today? I have to do something today. I want to have a big day today. I have to close out this week in a big way." It's as if every hour of every day of every week was a make it or break it moment. Not only the wrong way to grow a business, it will drive you to levels of stress and a lifestyle that is anything but enjoyable.

Now don't get me wrong: There is nothing wrong with that sort of positive thinking, and having daily goals is a good thing; however, those daily goals have to be the result of much bigger thinking and planning. You will never build your business one day or week – no matter how epic that day or week might be – at a time!

So you must start thinking longer term. Think about the two or three really big things you want to accomplish this year. Maybe it's 50 percent growth in revenue, opening a second location, launching a new product or service offering to complement what you already do. The choice is yours, but you have to think big! Nobody in the exclusive "Top 1% Club" got there by thinking small and playing small ball.

With these big goals in mind, now determine how you can go about making those a reality. What steps do you have to take? As with any big project, always start with the end in mind. Then work backward to determine the steps needed to get you there. Once you have that vision and understand the route you need to take, now you can set your daily, weekly, monthly, and quarterly tasks to reach your big goals. Now when you get up every morning, you don't have to ask, "What am I going to do today?" You'll have a clear and strategic plan about what you need to accomplish today and this week that is leading you toward your epic goal.

My example to fulfill our dream of living on our boat is a good example of thinking big, starting with the end in mind, and then working out the strategy to achieve it. Living and working on our boat is a big dream that has probably been percolating in the back of my mind for quite a while, possibly years. We plotted everything we needed to do ("How do we do it? What happens to the house? What about working so remotely? Will we have secure internet?"), and there were a lot of big things to figure out. We itemized everything and determined what we needed to do every month and week to meet our May 1st deadline of "setting sail." Rome wasn't built in a day, and our Floating Home will be a year in the planning and preparing before we actually shove off.

When you focus on the little, short-term things that aren't part of your plan to reach your big goals, it makes everything small. You can certainly do big and epic things, but you can't achieve them in short periods of time. Honestly, I don't believe anyone – including you – was put on this earth for mediocrity. We are all created for great things. Each one of us has the *potential* to create great things, but only you can convert your potential to be great into something amazing and fantastic.

Think about a packet of wildflower seeds. They sit unopened in the packet, representing potential to become beautiful flowers. Left unopened, these seeds can exist that way for decades – sealed in a pack existing only as "potential beauty." Everyone has "seeds of greatness" inside them, but like actual seeds, there are certain things needed to convert the potential into field full of flowers:

1) The seeds have to be taken out of the packet (their current secure comfort zone) and placed in soil – a dark, dirty unfamiliar place.

2) They have to be watered and the soil turns to mud – yuk!

3) Temperatures now go down at night and it's cold.

4) The sun comes out and it's hot, but the seed can't see anything yet and feels all alone.

5) Fertilizer gets dumped on it – what a smell!

6) Add more water until it starts the process of pushing out of its shell. It can feel the sun and warmth, but it's still dark and horribly uncomfortable by itself in unfamiliar territory. If you were a seed, I believe this is the time and space at which you most begin to feel your dream coming alive, yet it's still not there – frustrating.

7) Once it breaks the surface and starts to unfold its stem and leaves, everything begins to improve! I

imagine this must be like an entrepreneur getting their first sale.

As an entrepreneur, your journey will be like that of a seed: You won't go from the pack to greatness unless you go through the mud and the dark alone, being fertilized, and having a bit of a crappy existence – for a period of time. You can't escape going through the work if you want to be great and create your Dream Business and dream lifestyle. In hindsight, I now think of my first year in business, where I literally had no revenue, as my year of being put in the ground, watered and fertilized, and made uncomfortable and questioning why I left the warm and safe packet. But thankfully I did, and I endured the months of unpleasantness because my business truly has blossomed into my beautiful field of wildflowers.

When you look at successful people (athletes, musicians, actors, entrepreneurs, etc.), remember that you are looking at the finished product. You don't see the years of playing dive bars, waiting tables to eke out an existence, hours of sweat and training. You don't see all of the crap they went through to get where they are. You don't see their journey through the dirt to finally reach the surface and blossom!

Kick the distractions to the curb and play a bigger game. Doing big things is scary. You have to wait longer for results and you have to put yourself out there in a big way. That can be frightening. Sometimes the investment is larger as well, and that can also be scary. What holds most people back from thinking big and then pursuing a lofty goal are all of the what ifs that we talked about. If you want to achieve big things, you've got to stop playing small ball!

Affirmative Action Steps:

❖ *Jump and figure out how to sprout wings on the way down. Prudent? No. But if you don't try you'll never know how high and far you can fly.*

❖ *When you think of doing something big, it's human nature to immediately begin to play the "what if" game.*

❖ *Life is one giant "what if." If you fail, pick yourself up, dust yourself off, learn what you did wrong, and try again.*

❖ *Say no to playing small ball. Small ball never brings big results.*

❖ *Determine what big goals you want to achieve this year and work backward to determine the steps you need to take to get there.*

❖ *You cannot do epic things in a short amount of time. Remember, Rome wasn't built in a day.*

❖ *Your subconscious mind continually works on answering the questions you pose to yourself, so make sure you are asking for challenging things!*

What If...?

Chapter Five: Everybody Dies

Wow. Everybody dies. Certainly not a very uplifting statement in what should be a book encouraging you to spread your wings and see how high and far you can soar! Or perhaps you are still worrying about taking that leap and failing to sprout wings, ending with a splat, thinking, "Maybe Jim's right: Everybody does die."

That's not my point. I started my Dream Business Academy – Orlando with a video by Prince EA titled, "Everybody Dies, But Not Everybody Lives." If you aren't familiar with him,

Prince EA started as a rapper and has evolved into more of a poet after determining for himself that rap can be a very ego-driven pursuit. After a self-proclaimed spiritual journey, he began focusing on the "ephemeral nature of life," and his career blossomed even further with exponentially greater numbers of social media views and followers.

I believe his video that I featured at DBA speaks directly to the message I want to share in this book. While I can't share the actual video, I can share Prince EA's very powerful lyrics. (You can watch the video at: https://www.youtube.com/watch?v=ja-n5qUNRi8.)

"Everybody Dies, But Not Everybody Lives"

"It is not death most people are afraid of.

"It is getting to the end of life, only to realize that you never truly lived.

"There was a study done, a hospital study, on 100 elderly people facing death, close to their last breath. They were asked to reflect about their life's biggest regret.

"Nearly all of them said they regretted not the things they did but the things they didn't do.

"The risks they never took... the dreams they didn't pursue."

I fully believe this is 100 percent accurate. Will you regret not taking the leap because you were afraid to fall? No one wants to really consider the end of their life, but think about what you will regret most: doing... or not doing?

"I ask you: Would your last words be, "If only I had...."
Hey, you – wake up.

"Why do you exist? Life is not meant to simply work, wait for the weekend, and pay rent. No. No, I don't know much, but I know this: Every person on this earth has a gift."

Think about your Dream Business rather than working as an employee trading hours for dollars. Working, waiting for the weekend, paying bills. Your Dream Business is as much about creating time freedom as financial freedom. I don't believe any one of us is placed on the planet for mediocrity. We do all have a gift. What is yours? ***Just Say Yes*** to pursuing it!

"And I apologize to the black community, but I can no longer pretend. Martin Luther King – that man never had a dream, that dream had him.

"See people don't choose dreams, dreams choose them. So the question I'm getting to is: Do you have the courage to grab the dream that picked you? That befits you and grips you, or will you let it get away and slip through?"

What dream has chosen you? It's a simple question, but a powerful concept. King's dream was about freedom for all. I certainly hope your dream creates freedom for yourself... to do bigger, better, bolder things. Have the courage to jump and pursue it.

"You know I learned a fact about airplanes the other day. Now this was...this was so surprising... see, I was talking to a pilot and he told me that many of his passengers think planes are dangerous to fly in. But he said, 'Actually, it is a lot more dangerous for a plane to stay on the ground.' I said what? Like how does that sound? What he said... he said because on the ground the plane starts to rust.

"Malfunction and wear, much faster than it ever would if it was in the air. As I walked away, I thought, yeah, makes total sense because planes were built to live in the skies. And every person was built to live out the dream they have inside. So it is perhaps the saddest loss to live a life on the ground without ever taking off."

Are you sitting on the ground, rusting... letting your dreams rust? Now is the time to leap and head for the sky. Like the plane, you were built to fly, not sit on the ground.

"See most of us are afraid of the thief that comes in the night to steal all of our things. But there is a thief in your mind who is after your dreams. His name is doubt.

"If you see him, call the cops and keep him away from the kids because he is wanted for murder for he has killed more dreams than failure ever did. He wears many disguises and like a virus will leave you blinded, divided and turn you into a 'kinda.'

"See 'kinda' is lethal. You know what 'kinda' is? It's a lot of 'kinda' people: you kinda want a career change, you kinda want to get straight A's, you kinda want to get in shape. Simple math, no numbers to crunch. If you kinda want something, then you will kinda get the results you want."

Don't be a kinda. Kinda effort gets kinda results. Think big and dream bigger. You have to go all in. You have to do the work and expand your thinking. Like the seed, you'll have to be alone in the dirt and the dark for a while, but that is the only way you can ever convert the potential that's inside you into something really great.

"What is your dream? What ignites that spark? You can't kinda want that, you got to want it with every part of your whole heart. Will you struggle? Yeah, yeah... you will struggle, no way around it. You will fall many times, but who's counting? Just remember, there's no such thing as a smooth mountain.

"If you want to make it to the top, then there are sharp ridges that must be stepped over. There will be times you get stressed and things you get depressed over. But let me tell you something. Steven Spielberg was rejected from film school three times... three times but he kept going.

"The television execs fired Oprah, said she was unfit for TV, but she kept going. Critics told Beyoncé that she couldn't sing; she went through depression. But she kept going.

"Struggle and criticisms are prerequisites for greatness. That is the law of this universe and no one escapes it. Because pain is life, but you can choose what type – either the pain on the road to success or the pain of being haunted with regret."

You have to decide to keep moving forward. The stories of successful people are full of failures. Look into the history of any person who's "made it," and you will undoubtedly find failure, quite possibly many failures. As I said, when you look at success, you are only seeing the end product. You have to at least scratch the surface to discover what went into the achievement – hours of hard work and persistence plus the belief that success was fully achievable.

"You want my advice? Don't think twice.
"We have been given a gift that we call life.

"So don't blow it. You are not defined by your past; instead, you are born anew in each moment. So own it... now.

"Sometimes you've gotta leap and grow your wings on the way down. You better get the shot off before the clock runs out because there ain't no overtime in life, no do over. And I know I sound like I'm preaching or speaking with force, but if you don't use your gift, then you sell not only yourself, but the whole world... short.

"So what invention do you have buried in your mind? What idea?

"What cure? What skill do you have inside to bring out to this universe? 'Uni' meaning one, 'verse' meaning song. You have a part to play in this song.

"So grab that microphone and be brave. Sing your heart out on life's stage. You cannot go back and make a brand new beginning. But you can start now and make a brand new ending."

Amen. It's time to truly live. If you haven't already done so, decide right now to forgive yourself for any mistakes that you've made in the past and determine what you want your own brand new ending to be. *Just Say Yes* to creating it.

Affirmative Action Steps:

❖ *You'll never regret what you did, only what you failed to do.*

❖ *Everyone has a gift to share.*

❖ *Dreams choose you rather than the other way around. What dream has chosen you? Are you brave enough to pursue it?*

❖ *Airplanes are more dangerous sitting on the ground rusting than flying as they were designed to do.*

❖ *The scariest villain is "doubt."*

❖ *Don't be a "kinda" who kinda wants something because you will only kinda get results.*

❖ *Persist. Don't let failure derail your dreams. When you see success in others, you are only seeing the final product.*

❖ *The clock is running and there is no overtime in life. Decide to do it now.*

Chapter Six:
Seesaws, Leapfrog, and
Being Childlike

I've been preaching the importance and value of just saying yes to your dream. I want you to *Just Say Yes* whenever an opportunity presents itself, regardless of whether or not you currently know how to make it work. Say yes first and trust in your own ability to figure it out. Say yes and "go all in" betting big on yourself. Dream big and *Just Say Yes.*

Now before I go any further, I want to provide some clarification. I've shared my own journey and all of the times I did, in fact, *Just Say Yes*; however, there have been many times when I've also said no. It might seem a little odd, to stop here – in a book whose main message is to *Just Say Yes* to opportunities that present themselves – to suddenly suggest that you'll say no.

The important thing to be completely clear about is the reason to say no. If that reason is fear – fear that you will not be able to figure it out and fail – that's the wrong reason. If I had to summarize this entire book into a message that might fit a "Tweet," then it is: "Ordinary entrepreneurs become extraordinary entrepreneurs by stepping up—saying yes, even if you feel uncertain or unqualified at the time."

Life is about seizing moments of opportunity. Too often, just because the path forward is not clear, we say no to something that might actually turn out to be great for our business.

You have to determine the direction you want to take in your life and career, and when opportunities present themselves that are aligned with your goals, then, yes, *Just Say Yes* regardless of your trepidation.

If you get to a fork in the road that presents a path that will take you in a direction you don't want to go – one that will waste your valuable time and do nothing to advance your goals and success – you have my blessing to say no. As an entrepreneur, the decision to say no can be every bit as important as the decision to say yes. The entrepreneurial tendency is to jump into everything; I understand that and have been guilty of that at times as well. While I've been reiterating *Just Say Yes*, it comes with a caveat: Say yes when it will advance your goals and success *despite your fear*.

A Lesson from the Playground

I want you to clearly understand that whenever you say yes to one thing, you will have to say no to something else. Picture a seesaw or teeter-totter on the playground. When one side is up the other side is down. Even when there are no kids playing on it, one side will be up and the other down. Getting it to balance right in the middle requires two kids of the same approximate weight and a pretty good sense of physics and fulcrums. Very simply, getting it to balance is not easy.

There is also a balance in your journey as an entrepreneur, and when you *Just Say Yes* to one thing, you will invariably have to say no to something else. With a yes, one side of the seesaw is up and the other side is in the down or no position. If you decide that you are going to dedicate yourself for the next several months to creating your Dream Business, to taking the leap and figuring out how to fly, you will have to say no to other things during that time. You will have to prioritize everything that comes your way.

We all have the exact same 24 hours every day, and I'm not suggesting that by saying yes to the activities needed to build your Dream Business that you say no to something as important as your family – your spouse and children. Time spent with your family is critical, and I'm not suggesting otherwise. Only you can prioritize what is truly important in your own life; however, how much time do you spend on activities that can take a back seat for now? Watching television, perusing the internet and social media, golf, hobbies, nights out with friends.

You'll have to take a hard look at those types of activities and determine for yourself what can be removed from your calendar to give you the time you need to *Just Say Yes* to the activities that will move your entrepreneurial dream forward.

Just Say Yes!

Say yes to one thing and you will have to say no to something else. Only you can prioritize your life.

Starting a business is risky. Leading a business to higher and higher levels of success is also risky, and to some, achieving a certain level of success is enough. Some small business owners plateau – they reach a certain place and suddenly become much more risk averse, not wanting to upset the apple cart and risk the business they have created. If that's you, there's nothing wrong with that. Just be honest with yourself that you have grown a business that pays the bills and provides the lifestyle with which you are comfortable.

Who I want to address with this chapter are those entrepreneurs who are always seeking more – growth, revenue, prestige, financial freedom, and, of course, time freedom. A Dream Business is one that can provide all of these things and that typically requires massive and continued growth.

And that is where saying yes when you sometimes don't feel ready or qualified comes into play. However, there is a flipside to saying yes at these "super growth" levels, and the flip side is, learning to also say no!

Here's what I mean:

For example, you've grown your core business to high levels, and continued growth or wealth creation might mean looking for other revenue streams. Highly successful entrepreneurs are focused on wealth creation, and most "high earners" achieve high incomes by "cobbling" together multiple revenue streams. It is when we entrepreneurs venture into uncharted territory that we feel uncertain.

To be certain, I am in no way suggesting that you say yes to every opportunity. Quite the contrary. You say yes to every opportunity that has a better than average chance of helping you achieve your ambitions and goals, in life and business. So where does saying no come into play?

The one thing we all have in common is that no matter where we are on the income scale or when we started our business, we all have the same 24 hours in a day. While most entrepreneurs can learn to become more efficient and waste less time, there comes a point when super high achievers, if they are to continue saying yes to new opportunities, need to pick something to which they must say no.

I have a coaching client who has achieved his Dream Business. In fact, he has created and bought multiple businesses. On one of our coaching calls, he mentioned that his initial core business has reached a plateau and new sales, or at least the high level of growth, has somewhat slacked off. I asked when this started occurring, and the answer was about six months after this client had said yes to purchasing two other businesses. In addition, this client has also made a concerted effort to enjoy life more and take more vacations and travel more.

This client has put a CEO in place to run the primary company and, by all accounts, chose a well-qualified leader. Here's what I shared:

"In the first three years of your business, you were hands-on and very active in the business. It's fair to say that you also spent time with your clients and perhaps had some personal outreach to them on a regular basis. As you've been blessed with incredible growth, you've done two things lately.

"One, you've bought, invested in, or started three other businesses and made a conscious decision to enjoy life doing things that were once unimaginable. I salute that and applaud your saying yes to all of these things. What you have to realize, however, is that saying yes to these things comes at a price, and in this case, that price is a somewhat slower growth rate with the core business.

"Second, I don't care how extensive your search for a CEO is, and I don't care how great the training and incentivized pay structure are, nobody will care as deeply or as much for the business as the owner.

"So in this case, saying yes to owning multiple businesses and enjoying a life of travel and vacations means saying no the same growth and metrics you once enjoyed as a hands-on owner."

Another example is from my own business:

When I decided to grow my coaching program, I created systems and procedures, hired, trained, and empowered a team to virtually run my membership businesses – No Hassle Newsletters, No Hassle Social Media, Concierge Print and Mail on Demand, and Custom Article Generator. I believe I have the best team money can buy. But I also know that if I were in charge and running these businesses day-to-day like I once was, they would make me more money.

However, I said **yes** to growing an amazing and thriving coaching business, Dream Business Coaching and Mastermind Program and the Dream Business Academy, and by doing so, I had to say no to being actively involved in the daily operations of the membership businesses.

To try to do all well means to do none of them well.

So when you are faced with opportunity, whether a good opportunity or a great one, and you want to *Just Say Yes* – you want to jump now and sprout your wings on the way down, as your coach, I would tell you this: If this opportunity is going to move you forward toward your Dream Business and achieving financial and time freedom, then hurray for you and way to go! But... let's be realistic and think about what you will need to say no to as you are already maxed out on your personal bandwidth.

Again, trying to do everything well means nothing will be done well.

Say yes to massive growth, and to make that happen, figure out what you have to say no to, even if it is reluctantly so!

Leapfrog and Other Games

The digital age has warped our sense of time because things can happen so quickly now. It's like the old joke: "I bought my father a microwave because he was so impatient, but it actually made the problem worse. Now he stands in front of it saying, 'Come on, come on. What do you think I have? All minute?'" We accuse the Millennial generation of wanting instant gratification. Can you actually blame them? They've lived with it all their lives. Want something? Go online and buy it. You don't even have to drive to the store. Delivered right to the door the next day.

Despite the speed and ease with which some things can be done thanks to digital technology, you are going to have to get rid of what I call "microwave mentality." Yes, you can cook a hot dog in 30 seconds, but success doesn't happen in the same 30-second intervals.

Some things take time to build, and that certainly includes building Dream Businesses. You need to get rid of short-term thinking, and that includes short-term returns on your investment. Before I go any further, I don't want you to think I am suggesting that you don't concern yourself with getting an ROI. Not at all! You should be looking for an ROI at every turn in your business; however, they can't all be short-term. Chasing only those investments that deliver a quick return is microwave mentality.

In order to be truly successful, you have to look further down the road and delay immediate gratification and payoff. Think about stock market investing. When you opt for the short-term gain, it will always be a much smaller amount than sticking with the investment for the long haul. You could make $100 in a day, but wouldn't you rather make 1,000 times that amount over a longer period of time?

I will say it again: short-term thinking and microwave mentality will only ever bring you short-term and small results! You will never build a Dream Business with short-term ROIs.

Having said that, I also want to let you in on a secret: The road to success is not linear. We've all been subjected to that mindset throughout childhood. You start in first grade, then go to second grade, third grade, etc. I'm not saying that's a bad thing when it comes to education, but now that you have all that knowledge building behind you, you no longer have to do it step-by-step. There's absolutely no rule in building your Dream Business that requires you to follow a linear path.

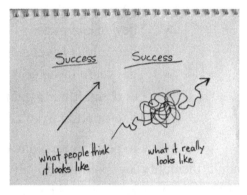

There's the current you and your business (where you are at this moment), and there's the future you and your future business (where you want to be). To get there faster, you can play leapfrog! You don't have to take every step sequentially. *Just Say Yes* to taking a massive leap. Study the journey that other successful entrepreneurs have taken and apply that knowledge to skip steps along the way.

The old thinking and mindset that everything is linear has gotten you to this point. Now it's time for new thinking to get you to where you want to be. *Just Say Yes* to leveling up your game and playing leapfrog.

Besides playing leapfrog, there are other benefits to taking a childlike approach to building your business. I'd like to share with you some ideas presented by Patrick Bet-David, an entrepreneurial mentor. It's his contention that the best entrepreneurs are like children, and I agree wholeheartedly. Here's a recap of his thinking about that concept:

- They're dreamers. Kids have fun believing in dreams, but as adults we tend to lose that flame of imagination.
- They never stop asking for what they want.
- They use emotion rather than logic.
- They don't think anything is impossible.
- They're always curious.
- They can quickly re-set their mentality when things go wrong.
- They're charmers.
- Their minds never stop.
- They learn faster.
- For them, life is a game.
- Their mindset is, of course, that of a child.

It's easy to point to each one of those ideas and defend your adult mentality by pointing to all the ways that life has been difficult since leaving childhood behind. There are all these responsibilities now and bills to pay. True, but I believe you will find greater success if you can leave adult logic behind and try to regain the imagination and wonder of childhood.

You have to re-light the fire and passion in a childlike manner to truly tap into your potential and creativity to achieve success. This doesn't mean childish, silly, or immature. It's a matter of working to recapture the innocence of childhood when everything was a game, imagination had no bounds, and anything and everything was possible! Study the most successful entrepreneurs, no matter their age, and you will uncover a childlike spirit inside that is driving their success.

As adults, many of us have become too logical to believe in dreams and to believe that anything truly is possible. Kids aren't that logical and neither are great entrepreneurs. ***Just Say Yes*** to fantasizing and dreaming about what you want to achieve because with the right mindset and persistence, anything is truly possible.

Affirmative Action Steps:

❖ *A seesaw is either up or down. Saying yes to one thing means saying no to something else.*

❖ *Only you can prioritize what is most important to you and balance your time accordingly.*

❖ *To do everything well means to do nothing well.*

❖ *Lose the microwave mentality. Building success and a Dream Business takes time, so start now.*

❖ *Short-term ROI delivers small results.*

❖ *Success does not have to be linear. You can leapfrog instead.*

❖ *The best entrepreneurs are childlike (not childish or immature) in their approach to creativity.*

❖ *Get rid of logical thinking and replace it with an anything-is-possible mindset.*

Chapter Seven:
Where Are You?

Where are you on your entrepreneurial journey or even in your life right now? Success can happen at any point in your life, but the only way it starts is when you make up your mind and decide that you want to achieve more, build or grow your Dream Business, and embrace your dream lifestyle.

No matter where you are, it's time to *Just Say Yes* and begin. I've already shared the circuitous route I took throughout my career and the path that led me to where I am today. Yes, there will be times when you struggle and there's hard work to do, but success does indeed leave tracks.

Age Doesn't Matter

No matter where you might be in your life, the best time to start a business and pursue your entrepreneurial dream is right now. As I shared in my book, *Stop Waiting for It to Get Easier*, there will never be a perfect time to launch a business... so stop waiting! The recent Great Recession and stock market crash in 2008 as well as the 1929 crash that led to the Great Depression served as the impetus for many new ventures.

Employees were suddenly laid off and with fear about the economic recovery, companies weren't hiring. The only choice – the choice I finally embraced after 15 long months – was to create my own business. If you are thinking of waiting for it to get easier, I assure you, you will wait forever. You'll be stuck on the ground, rusting and never realizing the potential that is within you to create your own success.

If you're a Millennial, you might be struggling to find a position in the career of your choice. You earned your degree, only to discover that launching a career in your chosen field is no easy task. Millennials are the largest generation in the U.S. as well as being the most well-educated. The latter statistic sounds great, but it also means there is that much more competition for jobs. It creates a stew of unemployment bubbling with frustration.

A college diploma doesn't seem worth more than a high school one as Millennials are taking any job just to have some income. Add in the average college debt and the situation becomes even worse. The Institute for College Access and Success estimates that 68 percent of graduates in 2015 had average student loan debt of just over $30,000.

It's difficult, if not impossible, to think about a dream lifestyle with debt mounting. Perhaps even the idea of getting married, starting a family, buying a house seem far-fetched because, very simply, who can afford it? Save for retirement? Don't even go there.

If you're in this boat, you can create your own future and one much brighter than you may have thought possible. There is a wealth of opportunity in the service industry in which you can launch your entrepreneurial dream and begin to build your Dream Business. Consider what skills you have that you can convert into a business. Perhaps leverage jobs you had during college summers. What may seem like a menial task can grow into a Dream Business.

Just Say Yes!

Figure out what skill you have, even if it seems menial, and start building your Dream Business on that.

Think I'm joking? Consider scooping poop – cleaning up after dogs. It doesn't get much more menial than that; however, there are several entrepreneurs who started that service as a side business and have grown those enterprises into multi-million-dollar businesses and are now franchising them around the country.

Certainly, you have a talent that you can employ, so embrace the dream and get started.

If you're in your 30s or 40s and have been in your career for a number of years, you may now be stuck in a rut. You're doing the same thing day in and day out, but there's little challenge and even less passion. Yes, it's paying the bills and you have a family to support. You've convinced yourself that the benefits, even if they are dwindling, are worth it. Maybe you haven't gotten a raise in a long time, your employer pointing to a weak economy. You fill eight hours or more every day, but there's a lot of frustration or simply a lack of joy. Sunday nights are filled with dread and Fridays are eagerly anticipated. You're tolerating it all because you've convinced yourself that it's better than unemployment, so you stick it out.

If this sounds like you, you are definitely stuck in a rut, running in the proverbial rat race, and trading hours for dollars. You believe that a guaranteed paycheck, no matter how much you dislike (dare I say "hate") your job is better than the unknown. The hours that you're trading away are the precious ones that make up your life. Is a tolerable job, at best, worth your life? When you get to the end, you will regret having spent your time that way rather than taking a chance and achieving your dream.

It's time to get out of the rut and off the treadmill and start working for yourself. It's time to *Just Say Yes* and start your own business. It's time to jump and find your entrepreneurial wings. There will never be a perfect time, and there's no better time than now.

Perhaps you are at the other end of the spectrum with a desire to supplement retirement income and continue to be engaged in a worthwhile endeavor. Sitting in a rocking chair is not at all your speed! Despite the youthful ages of the would-be entrepreneurs that you might see on *Shark Tank* or the young age at which the likes of Bill Gates and Mark Zuckerberg started their empires, there's no reason you can't launch your business, no matter how gray your hair might be or how many trips you've made around the sun.

There is no age limit on realizing your dreams! Consider Harland Sanders. You probably know him better as Colonel Sanders. He lost his job as an attorney (including, as the story goes, a courtroom brawl with his own client) and ended up as a service station cook. Of course, he went on to found Kentucky Fried Chicken; however, he didn't attain that success until age 62. Ray Kroc, a name you probably recognize, met the McDonald brothers when selling milkshake machines to them. He convinced them to let him franchise the business and purchased the company when he was 52. Does Chaleo Yoovidhya ring a bell? I'll guess not, but you've probably heard of Red Bull energy drink. He was 61 when he hit success and is now worth $5 billion (yes, with a "b").

Still not convinced? Consider Leo Goodwin, GEICO founder. He was 50 in 1936 when he decided insurance needed an overhaul and that he could sell to customers directly. Have you tasted Moose Tracks flavor ice cream? If so and you like it, thank Wally Blume who was in his mid-50s when he started his ice cream company, Denali Flavors.

Just Say Yes!

Age is only a number and no excuse not to pursue your entrepreneurial dreams. It's now or never.

Like age, circumstances don't really matter either if you have an entrepreneurial dream or, as Prince EA stated, that dream has you. Zelda Wisdom (that bulldog that started on greeting cards and now appears almost everywhere) was founded by Carol Gardener who, at age 52, was newly divorced, broke, and depressed.

It doesn't matter where you are at this moment – Millennial, Gen Xer, or Baby Boomer headed toward retirement – it's definitely time to *Just Say Yes*, roll up your sleeves, and decide that it's time for you to start pursuing and growing your Dream

Business and dream lifestyle. If not now, when? If you continue to "wait and see what the economy does," or "wait until the kids are out of college," or "wait until I've saved more money," you are paving the road to regret.

Dreamers and Doers

The world is full of dreamers and doers. There is no shortage of dreamers. They're everywhere. Anyone can be a dreamer, and plenty of people do just that – dream – without ever taking the steps needed to turn that dream into reality and live their dream.

Now you can dream about creating a business that pays you "just enough" to avoid being on someone else's payroll, but that is small thinking. Dream bigger.

Napoleon Hill said, "Desire is the beginning of all achievement." Desire is good, but it's not enough. How badly do you want to pursue your Dream Business? And your Dream Business should absolutely not be simply creating a job for yourself, showing up to "your office" rather than being a W-2 employee for someone else. Your Dream Business should allow you to live a life of freedom.

In my way of thinking, a Dream Business:

- Continues to grow even when there's a downturn in the economy.
- Has multiple streams of revenue.
- Becomes an asset for worry-free retirement.
- Is fun to operate.
- Always fires on all cylinders.
- Provides the lifestyle you want.
- Allows you to give back and make a difference to others and in the world.

You might initially start a business for financial freedom, but after you become established with cash flowing and you're not worried about paying the bills every week, there's another kind of freedom that becomes important: time freedom – the ability to do what you want when you want.

Maybe you're wondering how many times you've been at the point in your business at which you are ready for big growth, yet something held you back. Maybe the brass ring was right in front of you, but you knew once you grabbed it, you were going to go for a really fast ride… an acceleration for which you felt unprepared or that felt scary… going so fast that you don't know where you're going or where you might land. Inaction kills Dream Businesses! *Just Say Yes* to taking action.

Just Say Yes!

The top 1% have dreams, but most importantly, they are doers. Success rewards fast action. Procrastination is a progress killer.

The top one percent is made up of people who don't just dream but take action and do! "Hesitation" and "inaction" are two words that will never be used when discussing someone who is highly successful. I'm living proof that you can take a crappy mindset and overcome every challenge. All of the marketing strategies, business tips, and ways in which you can elevate your game mean absolutely nothing if you don't fix what's going on in your head.

Your mindset fuels the machine that drives your business. You can be the best dentist, accountant, engineer, architect or whatever your niche happens to be, but if you mindset is negative, you will never achieve the high levels of success that you could with the right mindset. What am I saying? If you're a dentist who is not operating a Dream Business or Dream Practice – it's not likely that it's because you need to attend another seminar on teeth whitening or how to manage your front-end staff more efficiently. In all likelihood, your position, branding, and marketing in the marketplace are not doing the job. In short, you see yourself as a dentist and not an entrepreneur.

The doers – the top one percent – are bold, decisive action takers. They are not the "WhenI's." The "WhenI's" are business owners who are not quite sure of themselves. When I find the time… when I save more money… when I do this… when I do that. They are also not comfortable with risk nor do they have the ability to take fast action. Success rewards fast action and ignores inaction. Indecision and inaction lead to slow-to-no growth in any business.

Entrepreneurs are as unique as people are, and clearly some have a higher level of tolerance when it comes to risk. To illustrate this somewhat simply, let's assume there are three stages of entrepreneurial risk, and I'll use money as the metaphor to make it easier to relate. The first type is the savings account entrepreneur. They're risk adverse. In terms of money, this type of person puts their cash in a savings account where it will be completely safe and 100 percent guaranteed but will return next to nothing. No risk, no reward. The stock market entrepreneurs understand that getting reward takes a certain amount of risk. When you invest in the stock market, you could lose some of your investment, but history bears out that you'll earn far more than the savings account.

Finally, there's the casino entrepreneur who takes all their chips and pushes them into the center of the table, betting it all… on themselves. They bet on themselves to win and win big. Fred Smith, who started Federal Express, is a great example of a casino entrepreneur. He went all in at a time when the economy was completely in the toilet with oil embargos and long gas lines. If Fred had been a stock market entrepreneur, he would have purchased a used Cessna aircraft and tried his idea with a delivery zone around Arkansas, Tennessee, and Kentucky. However, Fred went all in and invested in multiple DC-9 jets with pilot and co-pilot expense, maintenance crews, and delivery vans to deliver letters coast to coast. Fred Smith bet on himself to win big... and did.

Any Place Will Do

Even if you are not yet a casino entrepreneur, there is no reason not to start. While Federal Express is an incredible example, there are plenty of successful and mega-successful businesses that started in garages with stock market-type entrepreneurs at the helm. Consider some of these:

Walt Disney began his empire in a one-car garage that belonged to his uncle. Called The Disney Brothers Studio, it was located about 45 minutes from what is now Disneyland in Anaheim, CA and was the location for filming the Alice Comedies, which later inspired Disney's version of Alice in Wonderland. The next stop a few months later was a bigger lot on the same street.

In 1945, Mattel started in a garage where founders Harold "Matt" Matson and Ruth and Elliot Handler were making picture frames. From the leftover scraps, Elliot started making dollhouse furniture.

It probably won't surprise you that Apple, Google, and Hewlett-Packard were all garage start-ups. After all, personal computers don't take up a lot of space. Facebook started in a dormitory room.

But what comes to mind when you think about Amazon? Warehouse upon warehouse across the country, right? Founder Jeff Bezos quit his job at a Wall Street investment firm, believing there were untapped online retail opportunities in the book industry. He set up shop in his garage in Bellevue, WA and held client meetings at a nearby Barnes & Noble store because, well, you really can't meet with clients in a garage. He sold his first book from that garage in 1995, and the rest, as they say, is history.

Yes, any place will do, but you have to have the desire to start and the persistence to stick with it and see it through. For real growth and to truly create a Dream Business, you have to *Just Say Yes* and grow from being a stock market entrepreneur to a casino entrepreneur. You have to go all in and bet on yourself to win!

Affirmative Action Steps:

❖ *No matter where you might be in your life, now is the time to start writing a new ending by creating your Dream Business.*

❖ *Stop waiting for it to get easier because it never will.*

❖ *You can turn even the most menial task – like scooping poop – into a multi-million-dollar enterprise.*

❖ *Get off the treadmill, get out of the rat race, and stop trading your precious hours for dollars, working for someone else.*

❖ *Age is no excuse. There are countless examples of success stories created by those nearing, facing, or in retirement.*

❖ *You can't just be a dreamer. You also have to be a doer, willing to take risks to achieve the success you want.*

❖ *Plenty of wildly successful and big businesses began in garages or at home. Clear a space and get started.*

Where Are You?

Chapter Eight:
Just Say Yes to Your Business

I've shared my own story throughout this book, and now it's your turn to *Just Say Yes* to each and every opportunity to grow your business... no matter how uncomfortable or downright scary any one of those opportunities may seem.

It's time to look in the mirror, ask why that person is the single biggest impediment to your success and hold that person fully accountable. It's time to stop worrying about all of the what ifs that may come your way. You've already figured how to solve a ton of them to this point in your life. It's time to stop playing small ball and settling for small results. It's time to be as much of a doer as you are a dreamer. It's time to learn from other successful entrepreneurs, follow in their footsteps, and leapfrog to get faster results. It's time to get rid of a microwave mentality and trade logical thinking for imagination. It's time to forgive yourself, correct your mindset, and get rid of your head trash.

It's time to *Just Say Yes* to growing your business and achieving the success you desire.

You are actually closer than you think to creating and growing your Dream Business. There's a good possibility that you can't see that because you can't see what is right around the corner or the next bend, so your mind makes you think it's miles down the road and very far off. You believe you have to create something new or do something new in order to grow.

Many entrepreneurs suffer from this, and I call it creativity-itis. Perhaps you are afflicted. Creativity-itis is the belief that you have to create everything from scratch and must always be creating something new to get your business to the next level. Again, you are probably closer than you think. I was also a victim of creativity-itis. I stood in front of a high-level mastermind group and shared where I was at that point and all of the different businesses I had as well as what I wanted to create in the coming year. I felt pretty good about it. Then one of the top entrepreneurs in the group said, "You know what, Jim? You would be so much further ahead if you would focus on marketing what you've already created and do a better job with that than focusing your efforts on creating something new."

I couldn't see that and that advice slapped me right in the face! Honestly, it is probably one of the best pieces of business advice I ever received. Once I got over the sting of being rebuked in front of the group, it was actually relieving to realize that I didn't have to create a bunch of new things and could boost my profitability by concentrating on what I had already done.

Just Say Yes!

Beware of creativity-itis – an affliction that causes you to constantly create when you should be spending time focusing on marketing your current business.

So while I've been encouraging you to *Just Say Yes* to the things that come your way, it cannot be at the expense of what you have already done and created. You must find the balance, or you will get stuck in creativity-itis. For many entrepreneurs, creativity-itis is actually a way to avoid doing the things that must be done to grow a business. It's more fun and certainly less frightening to spend time doing the creative things rather than the uncomfortable ones. It was for me. I wanted the results, but until I accepted the fact that I was going to have to do all of the things that felt uncomfortable – until I jumped and figured out how to sprout wings on the way down – I was never going to achieve what I wanted.

The truth is that if you truly want to create your Dream Business, grow it, and achieve your dream lifestyle, you are simply going to have to do the uncomfortable things, no matter how scary they may seem. Let's face it: Fear is hard-wired in our brains and triggers the fight or flight response. It's quite normal to try to avoid the unknown because that is exactly what your brain wants you to do. But I'll caution you: That certainty that you crave is the same as the ankle shackle on the elephant. It is limiting how far you can go and whether or not you will achieve what you want.

Possible Outcomes

The most successful entrepreneurs know they have to tackle the uncomfortable things and commit to doing something even if they don't know how. They believe and trust that they will figure it out along the way. They know there is no perfect time and circumstances will never be perfect. If you are still scared to take the leap, still worrying about the what ifs, still afraid to go splat, let me share with you the two possible outcomes that great entrepreneurs already know about saying yes first then figuring out how to do it.

The first outcome is that they will succeed. They'll sprout wings and soar high and far. They'll achieve great success sooner. The only other outcome is that they will fail and fail big. Yup, they'll go splat. But they'll learn from that failure and ultimately achieve great success sooner than if they stood on the cliff, looking down and worrying about what if....

Just Say Yes!

There are only two outcomes: You'll succeed and achieve success sooner or you'll fail, learn, and achieve success sooner!

Successful entrepreneurs completely understand this and because of it, they learn to become accustomed to uncertainty. I know plenty of entrepreneurs who actually thrive on it. Perhaps they're also adrenalin junkies, but they relish the uncertainty and are, in fact, completely certain about their entrepreneurial idea. They know that taking action is the antidote to the fear that comes from uncertainty.

81

You're probably familiar with Whole Foods Market. It built its brand as "America's Healthiest Grocery Store." Perhaps you shop at Whole Foods, but I don't imagine you consider homelessness or living in a grocery store to be at the start of what is now a Fortune 500 company. It's a great example of two entrepreneurs who were completely certain of their idea. John Mackey and Rene Lawson Hardy, both in their 20s, borrowed $45,000 from family and friends to open a natural foods store in Austin, Texas. They ended up homeless after they were evicted from their apartment because they were using it for food storage for the store. With nowhere else to go, they decided to live at their store, Safer Way Natural Foods... without a shower stall because of commercial-use-only zoning. The solution? Using a Hobart dishwasher with an attached water hose. Wait. It actually gets worse: Less than a year after opening the original Whole Foods Market (after partnering with Craig Weller and Mark Skiles), the worst flood in 70 years hit Austin, and the store's inventory was wiped out and most of the equipment was damaged. The approximate loss was $400,000. But wait. It gets still worse: Whole Foods Markets had no insurance. Customers and neighbors pitched in to clean up and repair the damage and creditors gave them some breathing room to resurrect the store. It re-opened in 28 days.

I have no doubt that these entrepreneurs faced plenty of fear! Yet despite eviction, difficult living arrangements, and a devastating flood, today the company is the largest of its kind with billions in both revenues and assets.

You can overcome uncertainty and quell the fear with a plan. Think about it, develop it, and implement it. Determine what you want your Dream Business and dream lifestyle to be and write it down. Then consider what you fear about attempting to reach your goal. When you are clear about what your fear is, you are on track to eliminating the uncertainty that goes with it and can create the steps needed to pursue and achieve your goal. Make a plan and take action.

No matter what, the right answer is always yes when it's only fear or uncertainty that makes you want to say no. *Just Say Yes* even when you don't know how, then figure it out. This is the heart of innovation. Discoveries often happen by accident. Penicillin, microwaves, Velcro, and Teflon are just a few examples of accidental discoveries that made the world a better place. On the other hand, think about things like the personal computer or the smart phone – two things that resulted from their inventors dreaming about the wildest possibilities, saying yes, and then figuring out how to make them happen. Innovations like these didn't make the world a better place… they absolutely changed the way the whole world worked.

The Power of Zero

I first learned the strategy of the power of zero early in my business, and it's actually become much more of a mindset now. Early in my entrepreneurial days, I had a mentor who kind of took me under his wing.

Just Say Yes!
Start employing the power of zero, and you're guaranteed to achieve more.

When we were meeting one day, he asked, "So, Palmer, what's your dream? What's your vision?"

I said, "Well, it's very simple. I'm just so happy to get going and be starting my business. You know what? If I could generate $50,000 in revenue, I would be happy."

He looked at me with this *look*. It was a combination of surprise, shock, and actually anger in his eyes. He said, "What the hell? $50,000? Dude, think $100,000, $150,000…what's wrong with half a million?" He continued, "Jim, could you live on half a million dollars a year?"

Of course I said, "Yes, I certainly could."

He said, "Well, good. You need to think bigger. You need to add at least a zero to every one of your goals." And he challenged me to kind of tear down the walls, kick down the door... and stop playing small ball!

Your mind is a very powerful tool, but it can also be equally self-limiting. In my case, in order to generate my original goal of $50,000, I knew how many networking events I'd need to attend, how many people I would need to meet, how many letters I might have to mail. In other words, it was pretty attainable. I knew the steps needed to achieve that goal. But to make $100,000, $150,000 or a half a million dollars, that was completely different.

Now I needed to ask myself different questions starting with: "Okay, what do I need to do to make a half million dollars?" And suddenly over the days, weeks, and months that followed, it became very clear that mailing a few letters, shaking hands, going to networking events, Chamber of Commerce meetings, etc. wasn't going to do it. I had to think on a much larger scale. However, my brain was already working on solving the problem of "What do I need to do to make a half million dollars?"

So I'll challenge you in the same way. If your goal is 100 new clients, add a zero and make it 1,000. Keep asking yourself what you need to do to make that expanded goal a reality. Your subconscious mind will open up and will continue to work to help you answer the question and find the solutions. Conversely, if you stick with only finding 100 new clients, your brain will reveal the steps you need to take to find 100... but that's playing small ball. Don't do it!

Ways to *Just Say Yes*

As I said in the beginning: success leaves tracks. You are not alone. There are countless entrepreneurs who have gone before you, whose trials and errors you can study to avoid the same pitfalls and whose steps to success you can emulate to shorten your own journey.

The starting point is the degree to which you fully believe in yourself, your business model, and the product or service you're offering, selling, and providing. How much do you believe your business is going to improve and even change the lives of your customers? Will it make lives better or improve the speed and efficiency with which other businesses operate? How much skin are you willing to put in the game and put forth to really get your message out there and grow a big and profitable business?

I fully believe that you can purchase "speed" to advance your effort and grow your business faster. There are clear ways to accelerate your profitability. However, the equation of risk versus reward also comes into play. The bigger the bet and the risk, of course, the bigger the reward and payoff. Conversely, small bets lead only to small results.

Many entrepreneurs are afraid to *Just Say Yes* to a big bet and are only willing to make a small wager on themselves and their businesses. A small bet might be: "I'm going to read five business books this month on various topics." I love education and certainly am a fan of reading (and writing) books. But if you think you are going to read a book and implement what you learn in your own business, I believe that is the slow way to grow your business. It's a small bet. You are only investing $10 or $20 for the book, but your results will very likely only reflect that small investment.

The corresponding big bet is for you to attend a live event, even a multi-day conference during which you'll be consuming information from a fire hose with all of your focus on what is being presented, what you're learning, and how you can apply that in your own business. You'll probably hear from several highly experienced people who are sharing what the steps they took that did (and perhaps didn't) work. One or more presenters will be handing you the road map you need to take the most direct route to profit and success. They've already accomplished what it is you are trying to do. You'll come away with a handful of nuggets or elegant ideas that you can immediately implement to accelerate your business.

Again, success leaves tracks; however, it's a big bet for you to follow them in this case. It's expensive. You have to pay for the conference, the lodging, the transportation, and oh yeah, you have to step away from your business for a few days. Your investment is far greater than a book, but the rewards will be far greater as well.

Another example of a small bet is getting together with other entrepreneurs in your area to share ideas and perhaps commiserate about the challenges of owning your own business. You can cheer each other on and hold each other accountable. It's very low risk because you haven't put any skin in the game. There will be some benefit, but the results you get will be much smaller than those you would get from joining a paid mastermind group, especially one led by an experienced coach. It's that person's job to not only cheer you on and hold you accountable, but to really provide tough love when it's needed and never let you off the hook. Those things probably won't happen with your local gathering of business owners.

Just Say Yes!

Take the big bet and go all in. It takes a big bet to generate big returns.

It's a simple fact that, as an entrepreneur, you'll always strive to get the ROI. If you buy a $20 book, you'll want to at least finish reading with a $21 idea you can use. The more you invest, the greater the ROI you'll want to generate. The greater the ROI, the faster you will grow your business. You will be buying speed.

The right investment in your business can definitely accelerate your growth and your profitability. The right investment is the big bet every time, never the small one. The question comes down to how much do you want to grow and how fast do you want to create your Dream Business that will support your dream lifestyle? The answer is up to you, and the answer will dictate whether you place a small bet or go all in.

The Million-Dollar Platform

One of the things I teach at Dream Business Academy is the million-dollar platform that's needed to grow a profitable business and reach six or seven figures or beyond. It's a marketing machine and I fully believe in the results. I'm going to briefly touch on it here (the topic could certainly be its own book!) because it really does present all the ways in which you should *Just Say Yes* in your business, and it also represents some of the areas that most entrepreneurs fear or in which they are uncomfortable like I was.

I started my marketing with printed newsletters because that happened to be my area of expertise. So newsletters – both print and email – are a part of the million-dollar platform. Done correctly, your newsletter is the ideal way to get your customers to know, like, and trust you, and without that, they are never going to open their wallets and hand you cash.

Authorship – writing a blog or even a book – is another component. It is a great way to specifically share your expertise in-depth and also plays a part in building your own celebrity.

Podcasting is another way to build celebrity and share your knowledge. I really didn't know the first thing about it, but I launched my podcast program, *Dream Business Coach Radio*, and I share with listeners each week a few great nuggets about customer service, retention, and business building. I hated the sound of my own voice, but I just said yes and did it anyway.

Videos are the next part of the million-dollar platform, and by now you might be thinking, "Jim, if I'm doing newsletters, writing a book, and podcasting, why do I have to do videos as well?" The answer is simple: Your prospects and customers all want to consume information and learn in different ways. Some people are visual learners, so they want to see it, not just hear it. Some people don't have a lot of time to read, so they'd rather listen.

Just Say Yes!

The million-dollar platform only works when you employ all facets of it, no matter how uncomfortable some of them are.

Exhibiting, speaking at conferences, hosting your own live event or webinar are all components of the million-dollar platform. These were all certainly big, scary things for me to do, but I decided to *Just Say Yes* to these things, and the result has been exponential business growth.

I fully embrace this marketing model and can attest to its success. It takes each of these components for rapid and exponential growth. If you try to pick and choose from this list, you will certainly be missing or excluding certain segments of prospects because you are not reaching them in the manner that they choose.

If you want to pick and choose from some of these marketing methods based on your comfort level with some and discomfort with others, you are allowing yourself to stand on the cliff and look down. It's certainly your choice to allow yourself to just stand there, but if you do, you will never generate the growth you want and need to create and explode your Dream Business. If you allow yourself to stand on the cliff and look around, you will never learn to fly, and you will look back at the end with bitter regret for failing to do so.

Burn the Boats

It takes a lot of guts to launch a business, and I know it takes a lot of guts to jump off that cliff and trust that you will figure it out. I believe your chance to achieve great success is far better when you go all in. Another way to approach it is to not have a "Plan B"! Your plan has to work because there is no alternative.

Let me share a quick history lesson that was told to me by another really successful entrepreneur, John Lee Dumas, during one of my podcast interviews:

The year was 1519, and Hernán Cortés landed on a vast plateau called Mexico. He had with him about 600 Spaniards sans protective armor, roughly 16 horses and fewer than a dozen boats. He also had a dream of conquering an empire that contained some of the world's greatest treasure, including gold, silver, and precious Aztec jewels. By logical standards, the attempt to conquer such an extensive empire signaled that Cortés possibly also had a death wish.

You see, for more than 600 years, other conquerors with far greater resources who had attempted to colonize Mexico and take the treasure failed. Cortés knew the history and knew of previous failed attempts, so he took a different approach in his quest to conquer the Aztecs.

Instead of charging ahead and forcing his men into immediate battle, Cortés remained on the beach and worked to inspire his men with stirring speeches. He urged the spirit of adventure and stoked the desire for lifetimes of fortune. In coaching mastery, he turned a military exercise into an adventure in the minds of his troops. Through all of his oratories, it was a matter of three words that changed the history of the New World. Cortés ordered, **"Burn the boats."**

It was a command that smacked of lunacy: If defeat loomed at the hands of the Aztecs, there was no exit strategy… no way to retreat… no way to save their lives. There was no Plan B. Cortés was "all in."

Rather than undermining the confidence of his men, it had the opposite effect. With only two choices, ensure victory or die, it ignited the will to win. The outcome is recorded in history: Hernán Cortés became the first man in 600 years to successfully conquer Mexico.

There's some dispute about the veracity of this story, but it's not difficult to believe. A move like this would have (and very likely did) change the mindset of the men fighting for Cortés. With no way out and the healthy survival instinct innate in each of us, victory resulted.

Knowing what you now know about mindset, it's time for you to take the same action that Cortés did to conquer Mexico and ultimately enjoy riches beyond belief: Burn your boats. Cut whatever rope you might see as an escape lifeline. Put Plan B in the shredder. *Just Say Yes*, jump, and figure out how to fly on the way down!

Affirmative Action Steps:

❖ *You are closer to creating or growing your Dream Business than you think!*

❖ *Beware creativity-itis: the need to constantly create. Put energy into what already exists.*

❖ *There are only two outcomes when you take the leap and both result in success, but you gotta jump!*

❖ *Employ the power of zero. Add a zero (or two) to every one of your goals.*

❖ *Small bets will only ever get you small results. Bet big and go all in... on yourself.*

❖ *The million-dollar platform is a great way to grow your business, but you must use all of its components rather than picking and choosing only those with which you are comfortable.*

❖ *Be like Cortés: Burn the boats, cut the rope, and shred your "Plan B."*

Chapter Nine:
Test Me in This

Remember the "WhenI's" that we covered earlier? The people who insist they'll get around to growing their business or doing this, that, or the other thing when…. "When I have more time, more money, more whatever." They are the ones who are procrastinating. "I will spend more on marketing when I…." "I will hire an assistant when I…." "I will start delegating when I…."

These are the people who are always moving the goal posts because of life happenings and the daily challenges they face. The "When I's" never achieve their goals. They operate in the space in which they're comfortable, they never have real growth, and they never *Just Say Yes*.

What I'm about to share with you in this chapter is of a deeply personal nature. It involves money, spiritual beliefs, and serving others. I thought long and hard about sharing something so personal but what I'm about to tell you is perhaps the "granddaddy" of all the times I just said yes and moved forward with a great deal of trepidation and uncertainty. My saying yes to this has, without a doubt, transformed my business and my life, and in the end, I concluded leaving out this powerful story of my experience with this life strategy would do a disservice to you, the reader of this book. So here goes!

I'm going to propose something about success that is probably going to sound like something you have never heard before, and I suspect your reaction might just be, "Okay. Sure. When I…." I had that same reaction when I first heard about it, but it is a success principle that is so powerful that it practically guarantees a more abundant life and more success in your business. It isn't new; I certainly didn't invent it; and I've had nothing to do with perfecting it. I simply tried it because years ago a mentor suggested that I should.

I read about this from an entrepreneur who I truly admired and in whom I'd developed a great deal of trust. In fact, I chose to follow every bit of his advice as it related to marketing and business building. I also decided to apply it to my personal life.

The principle is simple: Serve others first.

When you serve others first, before you think or feel that you're ready, the blessings and abundance flow back to you ten or even a hundred or thousand times over. Yes, there is a faith component, and you can call it faith in God, faith in the universe, faith in providence, or faith in some other higher power. You can call it whatever you'd like. It flat out works.

Just Say Yes!

Serving others first is a principle that can change your business and change your life.

I've worked with many very successful entrepreneurs since I launched my own business, and I understand that start-ups operate "lean and mean." Once business owners achieve some success, they open the purse strings a bit more. They are more willing to give up their time or money to support their local nonprofits or charities that espouse causes that resonate with them. There's no argument that that's a good thing, but I will suggest that you put the cart before the horse instead.

Serving first – serving others before you feel you no longer have to worry about cash flow – is the way to accelerate your growth and accelerate the abundance in your life.

Freely giving away some of your money and setting it free to do good in the world – supporting the cause that is near and dear to your heart, whether that's a food bank, homeless shelter, building schools or supporting low-income educational initiatives, animal welfare, and the list goes on – almost always comes back to you in much larger numbers. Test me in this. It's been said that if you are a stingy SOB when you're poor, you'll be an even stingier one when you're rich. The inverse is also true: If you're generous when you're poor, you'll be even more generous when you're rich.

PLANT A SEED, REAP A HARVEST; SOW A GOOD DEED, REAP A BLESSING

Money Mindset

What would happen to the world, the country, your community and how much more of a positive impact could be made if more people served others first, helped a lot of people in need, and as a result of being a generous and cheerful giver, were then blessed themselves with more success earlier and faster in their own businesses? How cool would that be, right?

Maybe you feel like you have not one extra dollar to help someone else. Paying your own bills is a challenge every week and month. Paying down your debt is next to impossible. "An extra day or even an hour to help someone else? I'm working around the clock in my business." I get that. That's exactly where I was earlier in my life. I faced long-term unemployment, a cancer scare, and heavy debt. "Jim, can you...?" My immediate response: "No way, Jose. Check back with me later."

What would happen to your own life if, as a result of serving others first right now, you helped more people or advanced the worthy cause of your choice making the world a better place and, as a result of your cheerful generosity, you were blessed by the Lord, the universe, or a higher spirit with additional success? What if your business started growing faster and you began to experience even more success that resulted in you being able to help even more people, leading to more success for you, and a very

Just Say Yes!

Your mindset about money directly affects whether or not abundance flows in your direction.

positive scenario that continues to spiral upward? How much more purpose and meaning would there be in your life?

So put the cart before the horse. ***Just Say Yes*** to serving others before you think you are ready, not "when I...."

You might be wondering about my mentor who first brought me to this line of thinking. You might expect me to share that it resulted from faith-based teachings, weekly Bible studies, or countless sermons that I have heard since I became a Christian. No. It was marketing guru, Dan Kennedy, in his book, *No BS Wealth Attraction*. Yes, God does work in mysterious ways.

In the book, Dan relates an observation in which very wealthy individuals always saved ten percent and donated ten percent. Giving away money brings more of it. It works. While I'm not aware of any scientific basis, it may be a matter of mindset. You are consistently showing your subconscious mind that money isn't really a big deal, you're not worried about it, and you can easily give it away. When you conceptualize that money is easy to come by, you attract it. The key is consistency, and your mindset will shift when it comes to making money.

In my own situation, once I got going I knew that I could not save my way out of debt. I was going to have to grow my way out. I came upon this principle in studying Dan Kennedy, so no matter what my check book said or how busy my calendar looked, I just said yes and said, "Okay, I'm all in. I'm going to serve others first and trust God and the universe to respond." Admittedly, I'm uncomfortable sharing this much personal detail and worried about getting negative pushback when I first shared this in my audiobook, *Serve First.*

I'm not a financial guru like Dave Ramsey or Suze Orman, nor am I a biblical scholar. Yet I felt God continue to nudge me to simply share what I did and the results I got. I pushed back because the topic is not uncontroversial, and honestly, any time you interject God, faith, religion, or discussion about money into any conversation, you open yourself up to criticism and can become a catalyst for heated debates.

After one of my DBA events when I was in wind down mode, spending a few days just chillin' on my boat, I started thinking about how truly blessed I am. It made me wonder, "Why me? God, please tell me why I am so blessed." The answer came in a series of flashbacks about the things that Stephanie and I have done for no reason other than to serve first. God was showing me how the more we serve cheerfully and generously, the more abundance flows to us. I can share without a doubt that the less I worried about money, the more success I was blessed with.

I am convinced that serving first has 100 percent accelerated the success of my business, and nobody will ever convince me otherwise.

Go Ahead, Test Me

I felt God tell me, in no uncertain terms, that I was to share this information about serving others first so that those in my audience could try it and experience their own blessings and abundance in their lives.

It's the upward spiral: If enough people try serving others first, the more people will be blessed in the process, and God and the universe will respond with favor and complete the cycle of serving first in greater blessings. Go ahead. Test me in this.

My mission as a Dream Business coach is to help other entrepreneurs be more blessed with rapid growth and higher levels of success in their businesses. In the process, if this causes you to live a life of greater abundance with deeper purpose and meaning – a life in which you serve others first – then I will consider this a huge success.

When you start the cycle of giving and blessing others and you are then blessed with returning abundance, you'll get more excited about the impact you are making in your community or perhaps in the country or across the world. That is when your Dream Business becomes much more than a way of putting dollars in the bank. That's when your Dream Business leads you to more than a life of abundance but also becomes a life of purpose, impact, and deeper meaning.

This information has the potential to change the course of your business and your life as well as everyone in your life. Test me in this.

I believe that God is more interested in your heart and character than in your circumstances and that you must be willing to give freely and cheerfully, knowing you are making a difference in the lives of others without expecting anything in return. Once you make that connection, I believe that's when real blessings occur.

Once I was introduced to this concept by Dan Kennedy, I began researching the subject of giving and tithing, certainly seeing what the Bible had to say about it. There was one passage that was completely unambiguous and left no room for misunderstanding or misinterpretation. Consider the words in Malachi 3, verse 10: "Bring the whole tithe into the storehouse that there may be food in my house. 'Test me in this,' says the Lord Almighty, 'and see if I will not throw open the floodgates in Heaven and pour out so much blessing there will not be room enough to store it.'"

To me, God is saying, "Give a tithe (10 percent) and I will return it with such abundance that you simply will not have room for it. Go ahead, test me in this!" So I did. I started testing the Lord, and so far, I simply have not been able to out give God.

Affirmative Action Steps:

❖ *Imagine employing a principle so powerful that it practically guarantees abundance in your life and success in your business.*

❖ *When you serve others first, cheerfully and generously, it is returned to you countless times over.*

❖ *Put the cart before the horse – **Just Say Yes** and serve now rather than waiting until it feels more comfortable... when you have more money and time.*

❖ *Giving away money brings more it. It changes your mindset.*

❖ *When you conceptualize that money is easy to come by, you attract more of it.*

❖ *Serving first creates an upward spiral and the abundance returned to you enables you to give even more.*

❖ *Your Dream Business should be more than a way to add dollars to your bank account. It should lead you to a life of deeper meaning and purpose.*

Chapter Ten:
Life Is Short

Call it gaining wisdom, but the older I've gotten, the more I've realized that life truly is short. Yes, everybody dies, but you certainly don't want to be one of the people who dies without ever having truly lived. You don't want to be one of the people who dies with the regret of having not done something… not taken a chance. You don't want to be the one who doesn't jump and try to fly and then lives to regret that failure.

Failure is never fatal. Consider the words of author, J.K. Rowling: "It is impossible to live without failing at something, unless you live so cautiously that you might as well not have lived at all, in which case you have failed by default."

It is now time for you to take a deep breath and take a chance.

You were not designed for mediocrity! No one of us was. So now is the time to determine what dream is grabbing you. Have the courage to embrace that dream and do not let it slip through your fingers and become the thing you regret.

It's time to put a stop to kinda working toward building your Dream Business. It's time to go all in and place a big bet on yourself.

No Regrets

I sometimes wonder what holds some entrepreneurs from attending my Dream Business Academy or similar events. I wonder why they get stuck placing small bets and kinda pursuing their dreams. I talk to a lot of business owners who are on the fence about attending. I know the incredible curriculum that we offer at Dream Business Academy, and I say "we" because I always invite incredible guest speakers to share their own expertise about a wealth of topics that are important to every business owner from crazy effective marketing strategies and my million-dollar platform to dealing with human resource issues and even accounting tactics to reduce tax liability. I mean it is really packed with the best possible information that every entrepreneur needs to growth their business to levels they thought would be impossible.

So when I talk to business owners who are on the fence and not jumping at the chance despite the really incredible itinerary that will help them grow their businesses and explode their profits, I also know it's like the thorn in the lion's paw that is not quite deep enough to cause enough discomfort and pain for that person to make a change.

Maybe you currently have a business that is paying the bills, but it's not doing as great as you'd hoped or as you imagine it could. If you are not in enough pain or not frustrated enough by slow-to-no growth, I understand that you may not want to invest in an event like Dream Business Academy and its associated costs, including the investment of your time. I get that. I was there at one time. You're not sure it's going to pay off and deliver the ROI that you want. I get that, too. However, I'll caution you again to avoid short-term thinking about ROI and worrying about how quickly you might recoup your investment. If that's your thinking, you are failing to **Just Say Yes** to creating your Dream Business – the one that will support your dream lifestyle.

Just Say Yes!

Most entrepreneurs don't do the uncomfortable until their pain escalates. My advice? Don't wait that long!

No matter what your business may be, whether it's product- or service-based, I assure you the foundation is one of relationships. The things you learn at Dream Business Academy, once implemented, will definitely grow your business. However, that growth is like relationship building. It will take some time.

Will I tell you that your ROI on your Dream Business Academy investment will pay off the week you get back? No. Absolutely not. And it's ridiculous to think like that because that is really small-bet, short-term thinking and microwave mentality.

If the thorn in your paw isn't deep enough and you are happy with just getting by, that is your choice, and I do wish you all the best. However, I also believe with that particular mindset that you are setting yourself up for the regret that comes with failing to take action, for the regret that comes with failing to give it a try, and for the regret that comes with failing to embrace your dream.

I will say this with 100 percent assurance and in no uncertain terms, and no one will ever convince me otherwise:

Regret tastes like crap!

Don't look back a year from now, ten years from now, or toward the end of your life with the awful taste of regret. The only way to avoid that is to *Just Say Yes* to deciding that you want to enjoy the sweet taste of victory instead and start taking action right now.

No matter how long or short your life might be, don't waste it by living too cautiously and not exposing yourself to the potential for failure. Every failure has the potential to lead to great, great things. Don't fail by default because you stood on the cliff and never jumped. Bet big on yourself and take the leap. You will never regret it!

Affirmative Action Steps:

❖ *Don't be the person who dies without ever having truly lived. Don't fail by default because you never took a chance.*

❖ *If you aren't willing to invest in yourself, I know the pain of slow-to-no growth isn't strong enough for you*

103

yet. I also know it's better to invest in yourself and your business long before you get to that point.

❖ *An investment in an event like Dream Business Academy is not short-term. You will not realize an ROI in a week; however, the ROI you do receive will go far beyond what you probably imagine.*

❖ *The victory that comes with creating your Dream Business and living your dream lifestyle tastes incredibly sweet, but... regret tastes like crap.*

❖ *Right now is the best time to **Just Say Yes.***

Chapter Eleven:
Bigger, Bolder, Faster
What's It All Mean?

I started this book telling you about being inspired with a message from above. God was sharing with me that I should teach "Bigger, Bolder, Faster" at my then-approaching Dream Business Academy – Orlando. But the second part of the message on that cold January morning was that He wanted me, too, to step up my game by writing another book and inspiring the entrepreneurs who read this book to stop waiting for it to get easier and create their Dream Businesses.

As I write this final chapter, I just finished reading the manuscript (for, like, the 15th time!), and as I approached the end of the previous chapter, which I thought was the end of the book, I felt something was missing.

As the author of this book, I unabashedly said to myself, "Wow, this is an awesome book!" (Kind of like thinking your own children and grandchildren are the best!). But as great as the *Just Say Yes* message is, my gut was telling me that I needed to wrap this book up with "a little more" – put a big red bow on this gift by closing it out with a few more words about the "Bigger, Bolder, Faster" message.

And that is how this "new" final chapter came to be!

So, what does "Bigger, Bolder, Faster" mean to me, and how can you as an entrepreneur benefit from embracing it?

If you remember earlier in the book, I shared my memories of the many times I just said yes throughout my career… jumping off the cliff and sprouting my wings on the way down. The same lesson applies to changing your mindset from one of safe, doable, and steady as she goes to one of embracing the "Bigger, Bolder, Faster" mantra.

I'll share a couple examples as I once again look back at my own career for clues. Remember, success leave tracks!

When I started my first business in October 2001, I felt proud of myself for making the leap to become an entrepreneur. However, an early mentor of mine pointed out to me that I was playing it far too safe. I was trying to get on first base, where I could then figure out the safest and most prudent way to get to second base. His words to me were essentially, "Screw that! You need to man up, stop swinging for base hits, and instead swing for the fences, and I mean starting today!"

At the time, I was a member of the local Chamber of Commerce and was getting some clients from those meetings and networking events. Embracing what I now call the "Bigger, Bolder, Faster" mantra, over the next few months, I joined 14 additional Chambers of Commerce. I joined every Chamber that was within an hour or so of my home and was sometimes driving from one event to another, shaking as many hands and collecting as many business cards as I could.

This was the beginning of the growth of my first business by first, thinking **bigger** – not one Chamber but 14; being **bolder** – investing thousands of borrowed dollars that I did not have into membership fees; and instead of joining one or two Chambers and then waiting to see if this strategy worked, I joined them all… at the same time – the **faster** part of the strategy!

Another example a few years later: When I started my first online business, NoHassleNewsletters.com, I was somewhat getting used to the "Bigger, Bolder, Faster" way of doing things. For a membership business like mine, creating content and done-for-you newsletters every month essentially has the same cost structure whether you have five members or 500. So, slow, prudent, and steady as she goes just didn't feel right. As I've shared already, when I transitioned from my first small business to the more entrepreneurial online business world, I was only beginning to come out of my "play it safe" shell. Part of what was holding me back was the heavy debt load I was carrying. I wanted to pay off my debt, but as I've written extensively about this topic in *DECIDE, The Ultimate Success Trigger*, I won't go into that again here.

Suffice it to say that I once again chose the "Bigger, Bolder, Faster" approach... before I even had a name for it! I wanted to move swiftly from my first paid member to ten, and then 20, 50 and so on. This type of faster growth required bolder thinking, and it had to be done much faster than the pace to which I was accustomed. That's about the time I made two huge decisions: to join my first mastermind group and exhibit at a national marketing conference.

As I near the end of this book, I won't go into as many examples as I did earlier when I reflected back on just saying yes, but allow me to give you just one more powerful example of embracing "Bigger, Bolder, Faster": A few years after launching my coaching program, I was showing nice growth each year in both the number of members as well as the fees I was charging. But me being me (hopelessly impatient) and now somewhat used to "Bigger, Bolder, Faster" not simply as a strategy, but as a way of life, it was time to once again "kick this thing into high gear."

As I've shared "my most embarrassing moment" earlier, a very successful entrepreneur who himself had a multimillion-dollar coaching business challenged me, like nobody has ever challenged me, to essentially stop being a wuss and man up and grow my coaching business in a "Bigger, Bolder, Faster" way. That is when I started speaking more, writing more books, doing videos, starting a podcast, and eventually creating the Dream Business Academy. Any one of these marketing and business-building strategies by themselves would qualify for the "Bigger, Bolder, Faster" brand, but to the best of my ability, I chose to "go all in" and literally do everything I could, as fast as I could to create my Dream Business and live my dream lifestyle.

Was it easy? Oh, hell no. It was hard... all of it.

Did it make me question my ego, judgment, business acumen, and my very existence as an entrepreneur? Hell yes, many times!

Did I sometimes want to quit? I don't remember any thoughts of actually *wanting* to quit. But I had plenty of thoughts of wanting to "scale back" and retreat to a safer, more prudent lifestyle in which I didn't feel like I has so much on the line.

"Bigger, Bolder, Faster" can be scary. That's precisely why more entrepreneurs do not embrace this mantra. Not everyone is cut out to become an entrepreneur, and of those who do start a business, not all are cut out for this fast paced, put-it-all-on-the-line type of growth.

It is not lost on me that Stephanie's and my big adventure is yet just another example of "Bigger, Bolder, Faster." Could we do this journey in a year or two? Sure. Could we use the extra time to more adequately research the type of boat we should have, take more classes on navigating, learn how to know whether you're two or six miles off shore, and more importantly, how to find your way back when you can't see land? Sure! These are things that I sometimes wake up thinking about – especially finding our way back to land! That's a "What if" I hope I never have to solve!

But as I've shared earlier, life is one big game of "what if," and those who wait for the perfect time to act, to answer every question, dot every "i" and cross every "t" most often never do anything outside of their comfort zone.

Our ability to *Just Say Yes* to selling our home, putting everything in storage, and moving aboard a 50-foot boat for a couple years is the least financially prudent thing to do as we approach our retirement, or at least semi-retirement years. I can't think of anything riskier from a financial standpoint than buying a boat!

In boater's circles, BOAT stands for "Break Out Another Thousand" because every part or repair seems to cost about ten times more than it should. But I digress. We already said yes!

While the accountants and financial planners say, "Maybe buy a townhouse, invest in some rental properties, and put more money into the 401Ks," Stephanie and I said, "Not just yet. We have more life to live and experience, and we are ready for a big adventure."

That is our way of living the dream, embracing the "Bigger, Bolder, Faster" lifestyle that is very much a part of our lives as a direct result of me first choosing to become an entrepreneur 16 years ago.

So, what are you thinking about doing in your life or business?

What grand plans do you have, and have had for more than a few years?

If you could wake up tomorrow and be living your dream lifestyle, made possible by creating your Dream Business, what does that life look like?

And what is stopping you from taking a chance on yourself, pushing all the chips into the middle of the table, and betting on yourself to win big?

What is stopping you from creating or growing a business that will do more than just pay the bills?

What is preventing you from just saying yes and playing a "Bigger, Bolder, Faster" game – creating a Dream Business that will provide you the opportunity to live life on your terms?

If you're an entrepreneur with big dreams and big goals and you have not been able to turn your dreams into reality thus far, I have two suggestions for you:

1. Please read my book, *DECIDE – The Ultimate Success Trigger*. This book will fix what's ailing you from the neck up! Even though you and I have not met, I can say with at least 90 percent certainty

that the reason your business is not providing the lifestyle you want and deserve is not due to some strategy or marketing campaign that you need to learn. It is being held back because of the person staring at you in the bathroom mirror. Go take a look, and then read this book.

2. Invest in your business and the dream lifestyle you want and deserve by coming to my next Dream Business Academy.

Go to www.DreamBizAcademy.com to find out when and where our next event is. I guarantee this is one investment that will produce a fast ROI!

Sixteen years ago, I was sitting on the surgeon's table as he explained to me that my chances of being alive in five years were either 80 percent or 50 percent, depending on the outcome of the surgery. That kind of news will shake you to your core and cause you to rethink everything about the life you've lived and want to keep living. I realize all these years later that this event, as unpleasant as it was, was a gift and blessing.

Not only do I have my priorities more in line, but I also came to realize how precious and short life can be. As a constant reminder that life is flying by, I keep an hour glass on my desk... and am looking at it as I write these final words.

The sand, which represents life itself, is always running out. You cannot slow it down or stop it. And someday, whether decades from now or much sooner, the sand will eventually run out.

If nothing else I've shared with you in this book has resonated with you and moved you from a position of slow and steady as she goes, making only well thought out and prudent investments, to embracing a new position and higher level of confidence to once and for all get busy and play a "Bigger, Bolder, Faster" game, then perhaps this image will. Think about what's possible. Think about what your dream lifestyle can look like, especially if you were to create your Dream Business.

Finally, consider if you want to achieve this dream slow and steady as she goes, or "Katy, bar the doors; we're moving full steam ahead!" If, after reading this book, you feel like me that slow-to-no growth is no longer an acceptable option and instead you're ready for "Bigger, Bolder, Faster," then I invite you to apply to become a member of the Dream Business Coaching and Mastermind program. This is where you'll experience what it's like working with a no-nonsense business coach with a proven track record of not only doing this for himself but countless other entrepreneurs. Learn more at DreamBizCoaching.com and DreamBizAcademy.com. Don't think about it too long, *Just Say Yes*.

Affirmative Action Steps:

❖ *Honestly ask and answer these critical questions:*

  ✓ *What are you thinking about doing in your life or business?*
  ✓ *What grand plans do you have, and have had for more than a few years?*
  ✓ *If you could wake up tomorrow and be living your dream lifestyle, made possible by creating your Dream Business, what does that life look like?*
  ✓ *And what is stopping you from taking a chance on yourself, pushing all the chips into the middle of the table, and betting on yourself to win big?*

✓ *What is stopping you from creating or growing a business that will do more than just pay the bills?*

✓ *What is preventing you from just saying yes and playing a "Bigger, Bolder, Faster" game – creating a Dream Business that will provide you the opportunity to live life on your terms?*

❖ *Now is the best time to decide to **Just Say Yes.** The sand in the hour class continues to run out.*

About the Author – Jim

Learn More About Jim:

Jim's other books:
The Magic of Newsletter Marketing – The Secret to More Profits and Customers for Life

Stick Like Glue – How to Create an Everlasting Bond with Your Customers So They Stay Longer, Spend More, and Refer More!

The Fastest Way to Higher Profits – 19 Immediate Profit-Enhancing Strategies You Can Use Today

It's Okay to Be Scared – But Never Give Up (with Martin Howey)

Stop Waiting For It to Get Easier – Create Your Dream Business Now!

DECIDE: The Ultimate Success Trigger

Serve First and Unlock a Life of Abundance and Purpose

**Get Jim's Books at
www.SuccessAdvantagePublishing.com**

Check out Jim's popular Smart Marketing and Business-Building Programs:

Jim Palmer's Dream Business Coaching and Mastermind Program – www.DreamBizCoaching.com

Dream Business Academy – www.DreamBizAcademy.com

No Hassle Newsletters – www.NoHassleNewsletters.com

No Hassle Social Media – www.NoHassleSocialMedia.com

Dream Business Coach TV – www.DreamBizCoach.TV

Dream Business Coach Radio – www.GetJimPalmer.com

Jim's Concierge Print and Mail on Demand Program – www.newsletterprintingservice.com

Double My Retention – www.DoubleMyRetention.com

How to Sell From The Stage Like a Pro – www.howtosellfromthestage.com/

Custom Article Generator – www.customarticlegenerator.com

The Magnetic Attraction and Retention System (MARS Training Program) – www.MarsTrainingProgram.com

Interested in interviewing Jim? Visit www.GetJimPalmer.com or contact Stephanie@GetJimPalmer.com

About Jim

Jim Palmer is a marketing and business-building expert and in demand coach. He is the founder of the Dream Business Academy and Dream Business Coaching and Mastermind Program. Jim is the host of Dream Business Coach TV, the hit weekly web TV show watched by thousands of entrepreneurs and small business owners, and he is also the host of Dream Business Coach Radio, a weekly podcast based on Jim's unique brand of smart marketing and business-building strategies.

Jim is best known internationally as creator of No Hassle Newsletters, the ultimate "done-for-you" newsletter marketing program used by hundreds of clients in nine countries.

Jim is the acclaimed author of:

The Magic of Newsletter Marketing – The Secret to More Profits and Customers for Life

Stick Like Glue – How to Create an Everlasting Bond With Your Customers So They Spend More, Stay Longer, and Refer More

The Fastest Way to Higher Profits – 19 Immediate Profit-Enhancing Strategies You Can Use Today

It's Okay To Be Scared – But Don't Give Up – A book of hope and inspiration for life and business

Stop Waiting for It to Get Easier – Create Your Dream Business Now!

Serve First and Unlock a Life of Abundance and Purpose

DECIDE: The Ultimate Success Trigger

Jim speaks and gives interviews on such topics as how to create a Dream Business and live your dream lifestyle, newsletter marketing, client retention, entrepreneurial success, the fastest way to higher profits, and how to achieve maximum success in business and life.

Jim is a cancer survivor, has been married for 37 years, has four grown children and three grandchildren. He currently lives on his yacht, Floating Home, with his wife, Stephanie, their rescue dog, Blue. Jim and Stephanie love to travel and spend time with their family.

Connect with Jim on Facebook, Twitter, Google+, LinkedIn® and Instagram, and tune into his web TV show.

For more resources and information on Jim, his blog, and his companies, visit www.GetJimPalmer.com.

Subscribe to Jim's free weekly newsletter, "Dream Business Newsletter" and get Jim's popular free ecourse, "10 Days to a Dream Business" at www.GetJimPalmer.com.

JUST SAY YES & SAVE $100!

If you've decided that "slow-to-no growth" is no longer an acceptable option in your business and are finally ready to accelerate your growth and profitability, then I join me at my next Dream Business Academy. As a reward for investing in yourself by reading this book, you can save $100 off the ticket price by using the coupon code YES. Go to www.DreamBizAcadmey.com and when you register, enter the coupon code **YES,** come with an open mind, and prepare for growth.

NOTE: Seating at Dream Business Academy is limited by design. If you try to register and the current event is sold out, then please email coach@GetJimPalmer.com and ask to be put on the waiting list.

If you've DECIDED that slow-to-no growth is no longer an acceptable option for your business, then consider applying for Jim's Dream Business Mastermind and Coaching Program.

What is a Dream Business?
A Dream Business:

- Grows even during a crappy economy
- Has multiple streams of revenue
- Becomes an asset for worry-free retirement
- Is always firing on all cylinders
- Is fun to operate
- Provides the lifestyle you want
- Allows you to give back and make a difference in the lives of others

What Makes Jim Palmer's Dream Business Coaching and Mastermind Group Unique?

- This group is not for tire-kickers.
- Everyone in the group has been meticulously vetted before approval.
- All members come to the group prepared to give as much as they look to receive.
- Members participate in monthly group mastermind calls and get a private 1:1 monthly coaching call with Jim.
- Depending on your level, members have additional access to Jim between monthly calls.
- Every member makes a one-year commitment to the group and themselves.
- The Dream Business Private Facebook group is often a "port in the storm" for busy entrepreneurs building their Dream Businesses. Members regularly interact, post questions, success stories, and get feedback, motivation and moral support from each other.

Is this Coaching Program Right For You?

- If you're at the point in your business where you finally decide that slow-to-no growth is no longer an acceptable option.
- If you want to play a bigger game and are ready to experience real growth in your business.
- If you're ready to be part of an elite group of forward-thinking and action-oriented entrepreneurs.
- If you're ready to invest in your future growth and profitability.
- If you're open to new ideas and perhaps changing direction to achieve your Dream Business.
- If you're ready to create wealth instead of simply selling more of what you currently offer.
- If you answered yes to any of the above questions, then review the three Dream Business Coaching Options and decide how fast and how far you want to grow, and apply today!

If you answer yes, then apply today at www.DreamBizCoaching.com!

Get My Free Marketing App!

My free marketing app is getting rave reviews and has been downloaded over 8000 times! The vast majority of the content, what I often refer to as my Smart Marketing and Business-Building Advice,™ is free and you can use much of it to help build your business! It is available for both Android and I-Phone – just search 'Jim Palmer' or 'Smart Marketing' and get yours today!

I-Phone   Android

Made in the USA
Middletown, DE
24 July 2021